FORCED LANDING

FORCED LANDING

The last flight of a Viscount

Jim Rider

The Book Guild Ltd

First published in Great Britain in 2019 by
The Book Guild Ltd
9 Priory Business Park
Wistow Road, Kibworth
Leicestershire, LE8 0RX
Freephone: 0800 999 2982
www.bookguild.co.uk
Email: info@bookguild.co.uk
Twitter: @bookguild

Typeset in Adobe Garamond Pro

Printed and bound by CPI Group (UK) Ltd, Croydon, CR0 4YY

ISBN 978 1912575 961

British Library Cataloguing in Publication Data.
A catalogue record for this book is available from the British Library.

Find out more about G-ARBY and see reports of
many other local history topics at
www.otteryheritage.org.uk
otteryheritage@gmail.com

To
the memory of Geoffrey Whittaker and the
magnificent British airliner,
the Vickers Viscount

Contents

Preface

I am so glad that you have decided to start reading this little book here. So many people open a book, skip forward and ignore the 'Preface'. It is here that I want to tell you just why the tale of G-ARBY's last flight has fascinated me and why I decided to write it up and keep her memory alive. By the way, in most places in the book I call her Garby rather than the correct, but formal, registration code 'G-ARBY' because to me she has a real personality and has become a friend. I finished writing the last paragraph of the original version of this book beside Oliver Carter's field, at precisely 8.53 p.m. on 17th July, 2014. That day and time was exactly thirty-four years after the forced landing, for it was, in the strictest sense, not a crash. I planned to do that piece of writing right from the beginning of my project and soon after I had started the research. Those words appear, not surprisingly, at the end of Chapter 6. Some months before this day in 2014, which by coincidence was a Thursday, the same day of the week which saw the forced landing, I was standing precisely at the position at which Garby finally came to rest. This writing of the end of the book, I thought, would be a small tribute to an elderly lady, who through little fault of her own had failed to make that short distance to Runway 27 at Exeter and the safe end of her flight. I saw the writing of the final sentence as a small but fitting tribute to the superb plane, for that is what the Viscounts were. I also wanted to pay tribute to the many kindly and decent people involved in the final days of her long existence. I had long imagined her as a sort of graceful swan, gliding in over the River Otter but due to an odd disability her legs were tucked up into her white belly. But in my imagination now, I saw her as a graceful Viscount, lightly and curiously brushing, with the very end of her tail, the feathery tree tops away to the north, and then flopping with a sigh and a bump onto the dry grass meadow of Oliver Carter's field. Her flying career was over. She had died, rather serenely.

As her port wing struck the Lone Oak on her left and a spinning loose engine blade neatly dissected a luckless sheep, which happened to be in the wrong place at the wrong time, and as finally she turned, broken and bruised and slid towards me, her right wing leading, I realised again that this is a truly remarkable story. 'Hello Garby,' I said. 'Welcome back. It's time to take a break.' It certainly was.

Throughout the book I have faithfully reported many of the factual details as far as can be reasonably established now, thirty-eight years after the events occurred. There may well be some inaccuracies, but I hope these are minor. However, I have knowingly taken a few liberties with the facts and added some small, I hope harmless, details to help the narrative flow along. Most of these take the form of reasonable deductions and conjectures resulting from knowledge of the known facts and interviews with the witnesses.

Almost throughout the book timings are given using

the simple twenty-four hour clock, as this is what is used in the world of ships and planes and it is the most efficient way of clearly stating a time – so 8.53 p.m. is simply, 2053. Unless otherwise stated, local times are given, i.e. BST in the U.K. and in the air, and local time in Spain, which is one hour ahead of BST. Distances for flights and voyages are given in 'Nautical Miles (NM)' and heights are given in feet 'Above Sea Level (ASL)' unless otherwise stated as 'Above Ground Level (AGL)'.

I do regret that at the time of going to press I have been able to make contact with only two of Garby's fifty-eight passengers. They both gave me valuable information and confirmed that my account and 'reasonable conjectures' of the final flight are essentially correct. Our internet searches did register a couple of other hits and where we had an address I sent a letter, however these were either not answered or we received a polite 'gone away'. Many of the passengers must be out there but remain unfound at present. Perhaps more will eventually make contact and add to our knowledge base. We have a website open and a general search on the internet should lead an enquirer there.

Some of the characters on the plane and some scenarios are simply whims of my imagination but they are 'reasonable conjecture' based on the known facts. The purpose of them is to bring the situations to life and help the reader feel more fully involved. There is no intention with any of these inventions to portray any real person, living or not. I certainly have no wish to cause any offence. I hope the reader will forgive me for them and I hope that the proud memory of Garby is not diminished by the suggestion that there was a dead fly on her flight deck! The idea for the book came to me from a chance remark made by my friend and neighbour, John Brady. When out walking his dog, as he does four times a day, he fell into company with another man similarly occupied. As they walked through 'The Glen' in Honiton, to the south a Flybe plane was lining up for the final approach to Runway 26 at Exeter. John lightly said, 'I hope that one makes it to Exeter!'

'What do you mean?' replied his friend, 'Of course it will'.

'Well they don't all get that far you know. Some of them land at Ottery'.

Later in the day John related this conversation to me and asked me if I knew about the forced landing in 1980. I did not. Then he made what was, I thought, a curious remark – 'It landed on the cricket field.' Within an hour I was checking things out on the remarkable website Google Earth, of which I am a fan. It was obvious that John was repeating a myth. My interest was awakened and this little book is the result.

I do hope you enjoy reading this tale as much as I have enjoyed writing it. I am very grateful to the many people who have helped me and they are all listed in the Credits and Acknowledgements list. Now you are free to read the remarkable story of Garby's last flight.

Jim Rider
Honiton
July 2018

1

Going South

A turn for the worse / Trouble at sea / The magnificent Viscounts / A difficult day in the office / Counters and sums

A turn for the worse

Geoffrey Whittaker turned and looked out of the left-hand window of the cockpit. From three thousand feet over Torbay the distant Devon coast looked a little hazy and the storm which had been slowly working its way up from Cornwall during the day, causing small boats to scurry for Salcombe and Dartmouth, had not yet reached Berry Head. He looked back at number one engine, the port outer, as if by looking he could ease the anxiety he had felt for most of the flight. He turned towards the instruments and checked the fuel gauges again – something he had done many times since they had left Santander two hours ago. Again he cursed those faulty gauges.

The fuel gauges on the Viscount 700 series were displayed

down by the co-pilot's right knee so that the pilot flying the aircraft, and sitting in the left-hand seat, had to move his head a little to get a clear view of them. There was a gauge for each of the four, powerful, Rolls Royce Dart engines and at the moment number two was showing 'full', number one registered about ten gallons and the needles on the other two were firmly in the red zone, indicating 'empty'. Co-pilot Bill Hickock, known to all as Wild Bill, was not at this moment doing anything at all wild. In fact he was just waking up from a doze.

G-ARBY (Note 1.1) crossed the Devon coast, heading north, a little west of Beer Head and a few of the bathers splashing in the breakers off Branscombe beach looked up. Anyone at all familiar with aircraft in 1980 would have recognised the smooth lines, large elliptical cabin windows and graceful curves of a Vickers Viscount. It was indeed a beautiful airliner, and since it first took to the skies in 1948 it had been a source of pride to the British aircraft industry and the airlines that flew it, of which the leader had always been the mighty British European Airways itself. Geoffrey, being the deeply committed professional he was, knew just about everything there was to know about the aircraft type and one of those interesting snippets was that on its very first test flight the only thing to fail was a fuel gauge.

The route plan now required a slow turn to the west and Whittaker gently eased the control column over to port with his left hand and brought the throttles back a touch with his right. He listened carefully for the almost imperceptible change of pitch in the four turbo-props. Everything was normal as he concentrated on the approach into Exeter's

Runway 27 (Note 1.2). He asked Bill to turn on the landing lights and then the 'seat belt' and 'no smoking' signs, which Bill did. The Captain then asked for the Approach Check List and Bill read it out, as he had done many times before. They both knew all these routines by heart but flying regulations require formal calls and responses to be conducted on each and every occasion.

The flight, QA 7815, would safely arrive in about five minutes and then Geoffrey would be heading home to Jersey and Pont Rose Farm for a few relaxing days with Shirley, his wife. Now below he saw a couple of light aircraft on the grassy strip at Farway and then, as they came up to Ottery St Mary's East Hill, one by one, with a remorseless inevitability, the four great engines, exhausted as they were of fuel, quietly died.

Garby had become a 'glider'. They were slowly but surely going down and the wheels would not be finding their way onto smooth tarmac this evening. As the crest of West Hill, now clearly visible before them, rose slowly up the windscreen both pilots realised that it was impossible to climb over it. The scene was set for an air crash disaster. Geoffrey Whittaker and the other sixty-one persons on board would not be going home that evening.

They were just seven miles short of Exeter Airport and they were going down. Garby had no power, the fuel was all gone – the tanks were dry. The time was ten to nine on the evening of Thursday 17th July, 1980.

Flicking on the radio voice transmitter Whittaker spoke calmly but firmly, no hint of the panic he felt in his gut – even in this pilot's worst nightmare, he remained the true professional and called… '*Mayday. Mayday. Mayday…*'

Trouble at sea

Two days before the events in the air over Ottery, the 8,100 ton Brittany Ferries' vessel, *MV Armorique*, was just less than ninety nautical miles into its twenty-hour voyage from Plymouth to Santander in northern Spain. The vessel was capable of carrying 700 passengers and 170 cars and it was comfortably full. Although 'comfortable' is not always an appropriate word for anything floating in the Bay of Biscay, on this occasion a short swell was running and not causing much distress among the passengers. *MV Armorique* (Pic.1.1) was Brittany Ferries' pride and joy and although, as is the case with ships and indeed aircraft, there are often some minor failures of the myriad technical pieces of necessary equipment, these generally may cause some minor inconvenience but do not stop the ship from sailing nor the aircraft from taking off.

Armorique was built in 1972 and entered service in 1976. She was a good and reliable ship. Now she rests serenely, her life's work completed, at the bottom of the Java Sea where she was sunk in 2011, we think by design rather than accident, although Brittany Ferries are being a little cagey with the facts. However, on the morning of Tuesday 15th July 1980 she was steaming along happily enough, when one of her two massive main marine diesel engines developed a fault and had to be stopped. The Captain contacted the Spanish and French port controllers and after some discussion the decision was made to divert to the port of Roscoff in Brittany and the ferry limped slowly in on one engine later in the afternoon. After customs formalities had been completed most of the foot passengers were taken the 600 miles to Santander overnight by coach and those with cars started off for their homes or holiday destinations, with plenty to talk about en route. No doubt they would be claiming a full refund later from Brittany Ferries for the curtailed sea passage and other expenses.

Further south in Santander, the weather next morning, Wednesday 16th July, was warm and sunny but that was certainly not the mood in the Brittany Ferries' office – far from it.

When would *Armorique* be back in service? What about tomorrow's sailing to Plymouth?

Paul Burns, Managing Director of the ferry company, was not a happy boss this morning and had already phoned his manager in Santander from the company's office in Plymouth to discuss the serious potential problem of the

1.1 The Brittany Ferries vessel *MV Armorique* c. 1980.
photo courtesy of Jack

hundreds of new passengers who were about to arrive at the Santander Terminal being stranded, possibly for days, in Spain. These were passengers who had bought tickets for the planned 17th July Santander to Plymouth regular Thursday morning sailing. Providing an alternative ferry in Santander, at one day's notice, was impossible. How long would repairs take? What was to be done? Potential costs of fixing the engine, lost revenue and hotel accommodation for stranded passengers, were escalating rapidly. What would be the financial impact on the rest of the schedules and this busy, and importantly lucrative, start of the holiday season?

By mid-morning on Wednesday the 16th July the answer had floated in, seemingly on a breath of fresh air – they would charter aircraft. The suggestion came from one of the young lady staff members at Santander. The phones were soon hot as the Brittany Ferries' staff at Roscoff tried to contact UK air charter companies that might be keen to swoop in to pick up the pieces and do some quick, lucrative, business. By lunch time, two, and possibly three, aircraft were promised to Brittany Ferries and would be at Santander Airport by 0900 the following morning. Two of these were to be Viscounts provided by a company called Alidair, based at the East Midlands Airport, and another plane would be made available by an airline called INTRA.

In the ferry office in Santander there was a lot of administrative work to be done. With the holiday season just beginning the Brittany Ferries' members of staff were already at full stretch. Would they also be able to cope with all the passenger enquiries generated by the day's media coverage of the ferry breakdown? Extra parking for stranded vehicles and transfers to the airport had to be arranged and a flight schedule of some sort agreed with the chartering airlines. A UK receiving airport for the flights would also be required as well as transfers to Plymouth for those who wanted to end their journeys there.

Then there were difficulties of finally re-uniting drivers with their vehicles that would eventually be delivered to Plymouth. Fortunately it occurred to one of the team that the drivers of the stranded vehicles would need to leave their keys in the Santander office so that the vehicles could be driven on to the ferry. One of the interesting features in this story is that one of the drivers leaving his car keys in the Santander office was a certain Mr Bean, aged thirty-five, from Reading. Travelling with Mr Bean were his mother, his wife and their three children. Mr Bean was to feel jinxed by events for good reason and we return to his story later.

The magnificent Viscounts

As the main wheels of the very first Viscount left the wet grass on the airstrip at Wisley (Fix 1.1) on 16th July, 1948, its Rolls Royce engines shattering the stillness of the damp, morning air, aviation took a massive step forward. This, the first airliner to be powered by turbines (jet engines), was off the ground and aviation would never be quite the same again. The new Vickers concept, series 630, with the registration G-AHRF, was to become a world shrinking advance and one that would lead to the production of the most successful commercial British aircraft ever built.

The twenty-minute test flight over the Surrey countryside was, in the words of Chief Test Pilot, J Summers, 'very satisfactory… It's a natural aircraft'. Captain 'Mutt' Summers had been responsible for many other significant first test flights; including the Mk.1 Spitfire prototype and the famous Wellington bomber. Interestingly the only minor fault reported on the first Viscount flight was that a 'fuel flow gauge' had malfunctioned. Later G-AHRF's flying career was ultimately brought to an abrupt end when it crash landed too heavily during 'heavy landing tests' in the desert near Khartoum in August 1952. It may well still be there, buried under the shifting sands.

In 2008 as the last 'in service' Viscount drew up to a gate at Glasgow Airport it marked the end of an era. British aviation had never been better served by a finer and more reliable aircraft than the magnificent Viscount. (You can read more information on 'The Viscounts' in Appendix 2.)

A difficult day in the office

In the Santander office of Brittany Ferries the temperatures had risen markedly during the day; not just the temperature of the air but also the personal warmth of the three young lady members of staff who were trying their best to cope with the huge amount of customer queries generated by the news in the press and media that tomorrow's sailing for Plymouth was cancelled. By ten to six in the evening they were considerably hot, bothered and bewildered. So far today, Wednesday the 16th of July 1980, had been one of the worst working days they had ever had. They wanted to go home but there was no chance of that.

Their office manager insisted, firmly in his native tongue, that they all had to stay on and keep the office open. He then quietly stepped out and went off in search of something to eat and drink for himself; he was that sort of manager. One of the girls shed a tear as she realised that a planned date with a special boyfriend would now not be happening. She had bought pretty new shoes to wear on the date. The others consoled her and told her they liked her shoes. They were all friends. All the girls had been especially selected by Brittany Ferries for their superb skills in all the European languages and more, and they generally spoke English when they were working.

The office was situated, as it is now, on the quayside and had a magnificent view out over the blue harbour waters. Small boats bobbed gently at their moorings and larger craft made a tight turn in the main channel as they headed for the nearby docks. Two miles to the south the eastern end of the runway at the airport was clearly visible. Tomorrow the charter aircraft, which had been booked to take the passengers to Exeter, would be landing there from mid-morning.

After an hour and a half the manager returned to find the girls still talking on the phones to customers.

'Yes madam, you have been allocated seats for your family on one of our charter flights. Yes we do know you would prefer to sail in the ferry but, as I explained, there is no sailing tomorrow. You could delay...' and so the calls went on.

Now, feeling refreshed and more relaxed, the manager

coolly settled himself into his comfy office chair and scanned a telex message that was just coming in. To his complete surprise he read, *'Armorique engine fault rectified. We anticipate ferry will leave Roscoff later this evening…'*

He rushed out to the front desk and called to the girls in animated Spanish excitement, 'Hold everything. It's coming. It's coming.' Then he added quietly, as if this latest news might destabilise some delicately balanced political intrigue, 'They have fixed the *Armorique*. She will sail this evening and be here tomorrow afternoon. It's great news… we don't need the planes!'

All gabling at once, emotional and animated with the hot stresses of the day, the three girls immediately hit the Spanish nail on its head and would cheerfully have hit the manager in similar fashion.

'They can't do that. That is *so* ridiculous. We've just given out more than 300 tickets for the planes. You are such a fool! What are you going to do now? They will all be here first thing in the morning expecting a plane ride now. Oh my god!'

Two of the girls then picked up their belongings and stormed angrily out of the office leaving just one girl to deal with the still ringing phones. She looked down at her pretty red shoes and shrugged. She had the beginning of an idea.

The manager was standing there rooted to the spot. His mouth unconsciously impersonating a stunned codfish, his arms outstretched, hands open and facing the closing glass door through which most of his staff had just departed.

By twenty past nine the arrangements for the passengers had been sorted out for the following day by the remaining girl with the pretty shoes. What a treasure she was proving to be. Even the generally thoughtless and unappreciative manager had seen her as his saviour.

He realised that if things did not go well tomorrow he would be in trouble much deeper than the waters outside his office. The Head of Operations in England would be after his Spanish blood. He was not ignorant of all of his country's maritime history. There was nothing unusual about the English giving the Spanish a 'good licking'.

The remaining girl had had what she thought to be a good idea; the only morsel of pleasure to come her way today she thought. Her last call was made quietly and privately as it was to her boyfriend, the current big love in her life.

'I've checked all the passenger lists for the flights tomorrow. The last flight leaves at half past seven and has only fifty-six on board – that leaves five spare seats. I've worked a double shift today and I'm due time off. I'm holding seats for the two of us. You'll need to be here to check-in by quarter to seven in the evening. Is that alright?'

'Oh yes, yes!' came the excited reply.

They were going to be on the plane and they were heading for a view of Devon's green fields; well certainly one in particular.

At 2300, 400 miles to the north, against all the odds, and to the grave inconvenience of the Santander office team, the magnificent, now fully functional, *MV Armorique*, its port engine purring away as if it could never possibly be a nuisance to anyone, sailed serenely out of Roscoff harbour and turned west. The evening tide was setting and most of the passengers were long departed. She set a course for

Santander and the unusually serene vessel would arrive there in a little over sixteen hours.

Counters and sums

The next morning, Thursday 17th July 1980, the three chartered aircraft began the planned shuttle schedule. Garby left Exeter, climbing through the early cloud, as did the other Alidair aircraft on the charter, Viscount 815 G-AVJB a little later. Garby made an uneventful first trip down to Santander in good weather and returned with probably a full load of around sixty passengers at the end of the morning.

This was the first of Garby's round trips but the crew for this morning flight were not Whittaker and Hickock but a different crew. Garby returned to Exeter about forty minutes late, soon after 1330(BST). The reason for the delay was that at around 1045 there had been a minor problem on the ground at Santander when the electrical power supply, powering the fuel loading pump, had become defective. This had caused Garby's refuelling valve to open and close intermittently and as a result the refuelling process was interrupted. The counters on the refuelling bowser ceased to turn each time the supply stopped so the malfunction was easily detected on the meters. The possibility exists, however, that the pump may have been misused, or adjusted in some way, and that could have caused the malfunction. Later in the day Geoffrey Whittaker, using very strong language in the passenger cabin on the aircraft after the landing, vehemently and specifically blamed the Spanish for '… not filling me up properly!' He also intimated that the Spanish bowser crew might both have been conceived out of wedlock!

The fresh crew signed on for duty at Exeter at 1215 and waited for Garby's return. These Alidair employees were the aircraft commander, Captain Geoffrey Whittaker, aged fifty-five from Jersey, Co-Pilot Bill Hickock, aged fifty-eight and two stewardesses, Sue Hudson and Sandra McNeil. This crew had worked together on many occasions and the two pilots knew each other well. Geoff was a veteran pilot with more than 14,000 flying hours logged and Bill had piloted for just less than 4,000 hours. However Garby was the real veteran of the piece and at this point in her career she had flown more than 35,000 hours and landed well in excess of 29,000 times. It will come as no surprise to the layman that one of the key principles of aviation is that the number of take offs should be matched by the same number of landings. So far Garby had achieved a perfectly matched score but there was plenty of flying time left on this fateful Thursday.

It is a fact that aviators are always doing sums. Numbers, maths, calculations, estimates, equations and quantities are the fundamentals by which aeroplanes stay in the air and pilots get them up and down and in the right place on the ground. If you can't do maths you can't ever be a pilot. Some of the maths are very complicated and some are well within the capabilities of a bright Primary School child. Nowadays most of the maths – the only exception being whether or not the pilot wants one lump or two in his tea – is done by a computer or two, or even three, but in 1980 the pilots did the sums.

Recently my daughter was in an aircraft and about to take off from New York's JFK Airport, when one of the three on-board computers failed. The flight returned to the gate and was then out of service for fifteen hours. That would not have happened in 1980.

When I was researching for this book I was interviewing two pilots and I lightly asked, '… so what would have been Garby's stalling speed?' This basic information is always given in the handbook that comes with your airliner when you buy it of course, but if you lose the handbook then you will need to work it out. My pilots had clearly not read the Viscount handbook so they mumbled to themselves for about ten seconds along the lines of '493 times 0.086 by the height… air pressure at 29.92 *mumble, mumble…* ah, 84 knots!' they said together and nodded in a knowing sort of way.

I was impressed, really impressed, because my small brain does not work that way. Anyway, statistics are the bread and butter of everything aircraft one way or another so – as you will want to know what really happened to Garby later on this fateful Thursday – it is now necessary to start inflicting a few of these stats on you. I hope you are steeled for them!

I need to begin with Garby's capacity for juice; how many litres of fuel did she need for her flight? Ultimately something went wrong, somewhere, with the fuel quantity on board and that is why her nose finished up in a field exactly 4.94 miles (Fix 1.2) from where it would have been if she had made it to Runway 27 at Exeter Airport (Fix

1.3). There are four fuel tanks – but actually they were fuel bladders – one for each engine. They are located in the wings. When full they can accommodate together 6,256 litres – interestingly, that's about 150 car-fulls, ouch! There is a pumping system for shifting the fuel around to keep the aircraft balanced as it flies a bit better that way, rather than leaning over to one side, in which case it likes to permanently go round an imaginary corner. Oh, and by the way, just to confuse you some more, in 1980 all fuel measurements in the UK were in gallons not litres, but the continentals measured fuel in litres, not gallons. Some scope for error there then.

Before taking off on the second outward flight of the day, which would have just the four crew on board, the ground fuel staff at Exeter delivered, according to the pilot's instruction, enough fuel for full tanks. Consequently 4,430 litres were loaded and this, added to the 1,793 remaining after the previous flight, gave the on-board total before departure from Exeter as 6,223 litres, just a little short of full. By the way, to save you running for your calculator, in today's (mid 2018) prices that's around £8,000 worth. They had plenty to make the trip down to Spain and also had the statutory diversionary fuel for an extra ninety minutes of flying plus another 10% just to be on the safe side. The time was 1415.

Usually the pilot will choose to fly on the four available engines and sets the four independent throttle levers to the same setting. Provided the engines are working correctly the amount of fuel burnt by each engine should be about the same and, therefore, at the end of a flight the amount of fuel remaining in the four main tanks will be almost the same. Trim can easily be upset by a moving passenger and pumping some fuel around can easily even up the delicate balance.

As every-day big aircraft are flying over our heads it would be reassuring to think that both the aircraft captain and the co-pilot stand beside the fuel bowser watching the man filling her up and seeing the needles spinning around as the fuel goes in, just as we do on the garage forecourt. Alas no, it doesn't work quite that way. The pilot is often somewhere else working out some sum or other, like the wind speed over Wapping High Street, the distance to Naples, or what the Jet Stream is thinking of doing next week. Overseeing the fuelling is often left to the co-pilot but co-pilots can, and do, or at least this one did, often sit in the dry cockpit reading a book and then pop down and sign on the log sheet that the fuel has been fully loaded. Some more scope for error there. The airline will eventually pay for the fuel based on that signature and indeed Garby's fuel taken on at Exeter, and later at Santander, was properly signed for by co-pilot Bill Hickock.

An uneventful flight south, taking a little over two hours for the 470 nautical mile trip, brought Garby into Santander Airport eight minutes ahead of schedule at 1822 local time. Bill was the pilot for this leg and the aircraft commander, Geoff Whittaker, acted as co-pilot and sat in the right-hand seat. This was, and is, a perfectly normal procedure. The captain of the aircraft does not have to be the pilot flying it but the Captain, alternatively known as the commander, has overall responsibility.

If Captain Geoff Whittaker had looked down to his right as Bill brought the plane into land on Santander's Runway 29 he might have noticed a smart large white ferry tied up along the seafront. It was the *Armorique*.

After they had landed the crew were able to have a meal and a short rest period before finalising arrangements for the return flight. More sums. Captain Geoff went to the flight office to take care of the paperwork and administration and probably talk to the ferry line. Out on the airfield the Spanish bowser arrived to fuel the plane.

Trouble was on the wing. Garby's number was up and lamb chops were on Friday's menu.

1.2(above): Viscount V701 cabin c.1980. G-ALWF, photographed at Duxford. 1.3(below): Pilot's seat position on a Viscount V701 G-ALWF, photographed at Duxford.
(Pictures; Jim Rider 2014)

1.4: Flight deck view. Viscount V701 G-ALWF, photographed at Duxford. Note position of fuel gauges below right-hand yoke.
(Picture; Jim Rider 2014)

2

Going North

Fill her up / Heading home / Flight Deck visitors / Geoffrey / More Flight Deck unease

Fill her up

In the late afternoon the warm Spanish air was balmy and full of the heady aroma of sweet smelling mimosa. Quite where this intoxicating fragrance was coming from was unclear to Bill Hickock as he sat lazily in Garby's cockpit. He was in the captain's seat, on the left side, and the small window by his shoulder was open. Between short catnaps he was slowly reading pages from the novel on his lap. He had a bit of a penchant for Ian Fleming and he was working through a James Bond *Goldfinger*. But another smell was in the air, a smell with which he was thoroughly familiar, 'AVTUR' – AViation TURbine fuel – no one working around planes could mistake it. A few metres below him the fuel bowser was delivering its load to the aircraft and it was Bill's duty to check the uplift and that was what he was, well, sort of doing. When the bowser arrived earlier he had ordered 2,720 litres and then he wrote the figures down and showed them to the senior bowser operator to avoid the possibility of any language confusion. Bill did not claim to be a confident and fluent linguist.

The bowser driver uncoupled the hose from the right wing and manoeuvred the vehicle around the nose to the left. Bill watched as the other operator first reconnected the electrical power cable and then the same fuel hose that he had just used on the right wing. He then opened the fuel flow valve. Bill was content that fuel was being loaded correctly. Everything smelt and sounded normal.

The power for this uplift was being supplied by the aircraft's batteries because on the previous flight the ground power supply to the bowser had been thought to be erratic by the bowser operators. The aircraft was now in turn being powered from a nearby ground power unit. This was working properly and had already been used by Garby's first crew of the day when they had made their trip down to Spain in the morning. However the bowser and its crew were different to those provided to service that previous flight, but this may not have been known to Bill and Geoff.

All these details are significant because somewhere, something went wrong with this fuel uplift. What the mistake, error or malpractice – or whatever the combination of those might actually have been – was not fully decided in the subsequent Air Accident Investigation Branch (AAIB) report (Apx 1). However, Bill was satisfied that as far as he could tell everything was in order. He was, after all, about to fly in Garby and despite the nearly 4,000 pilot hours he had flown he never forgot the risks. He knew that his life and the lives of everyone else on the flight depended on this fuel and the safe operation of the aircraft itself, but there was in the background, what can only be described as a niggling 'terminology' issue.

To be scrupulously fair to Bill, Geoff and the anonymous bowser operators, in 1980 there was a general lack of standardization in the way units of weight and capacity were measured in the aircraft industry. This multiplicity in itself was enough to cause confusion and more importantly, give scope for error. See how you get on with these: the aircraft's tank capacity was measured in imperial gallons; the fuel flows indicated in gauges on the flight deck may have been in lbs (pounds weight) or gallons; the bowser's gauges in Santander were metric (litres) and the fuel weight calculation for the aircraft weight and balance in the 'load sheet' would have been in kilograms. Confusing? Well it certainly baffles me! This is the 'unit terminology environment' in which the pilot had to make the important calculations that are fundamental to the safety of the flight. Is it any wonder things sometimes went wrong?

In the warm cockpit Bill nodded a few times and was soon happily away with the fairies, lulled to sleep for a few minutes by the sweet smells and the gentle hum of the pumps. All was well but he was tired from an early start and the physical effort of the flight leg he had just flown from Exeter. He had been the 'pilot handling' but for the return leg he would be the 'pilot not handling'. His job on the way home would be to monitor everything, including the weather, navigation and fuel flow, and leave the flying to the 'pilot handling', Captain Geoff Whittaker.

A seemingly minor point to be made here is that both pilots were fully qualified and very experienced captains. This should not have had any influence on their professional conduct in the air but human psychology might have played a part and influenced the decision-making process, resulting in bad choices being taken by the 'pilot handling' the homeward leg.

Garby was in reasonable nick for an old girl – perhaps a little worn around the edges with tell-tale signs of old age showing in her fundamentals. Her external paintwork was, after all, only three years old for she had come back into the Alidair family from Dan Air in 1977. Previously she had been owned by British United and a number of other lines. She was a grand old lady of the airways. But she did have her annoying little foibles as both Bill and Geoff well knew.

Things were not quite as they should have been, mechanically and electrically speaking, but very few aircraft, then and indeed now, take off in a state of technical perfection, which is perhaps a little worrying for us modern jetsetters. Garby had a secret – a Loch Ness sort of secret – so deep and dark that not even her expert mechanics back at East Midlands could ever fathom its true depth and origin. It was a 'let's try our best to find out how much fuel is actually in your tanks old girl' sort of secret, and she would never tell. To her the amount of fuel she had tucked away was her business and very, very private. No matter how many times her pilots tweaked her knobs, tickled her dials and called her all sorts of hurtful and unladylike names, those fuel gauges usually spoke with forked tongue and the pilots' calculations of the actual amount of fuel on board was generally made with a measure of optimistic caution. It was an estimate in fact, not a fact, in fact. That was certainly the case on this flight, as we are soon to discover. The defects were recorded in the aircraft's technical log but Bill was not fully aware of the details. Bill was again to remark those delicate choice words that summed up the situation succinctly but with a disarming lack of subtlety –

'The old cow's at it again!'

Bill was suddenly woken by a thump on the forward door frame and a cheery shout from Carlos, the senior of the two bowser operators.

'You sign now pleeeze! Is done.'

Bill grumbled under his breath, squeezed out of his seat, avoided banging his head on the top dials and went down the front eleven steps to the tarmac.

'How much have you loaded?'

In response Carlos took him to the side of the bowser and showed him the dials. Satisfied that the requested upload of 2720 litres had been made, Bill signed the delivery note. It was Garby's death warrant.

Captain Geoff Whittaker was at this moment – around 1850 – nearby in an office completing his flight plan (Pic 2.1) and checking through weather reports. This flight plan stated his intended route and included his departure and destination aerodromes, timings, alternative destinations, route, total endurance fuel and as the route was over water, that yellow dinghies with life jackets were being carried! All the key information was there. Garby's intended route was Santander direct (DCT) to Cognac VOR (CGC) then join A25 and on to – Nantes (NTS), Dinard (DIN), the Skerry Reporting Point (RP), south-east of Berry Head then finally, Exeter. An aircraft can join an 'airway' at any of the reporting points along it and this is what Garby did (Apx 8).

The other two members of the aircraft's four crew, the two stewardesses Sue and Sandra, were checking the passenger list ready for boarding, which they were planning to commence at around 1900 ready for the planned 1930 'off the blocks' (from the terminal) departure. In Exeter the time for this departure was 1830 British Summer Time. Previously, before fuelling had commenced, Geoffrey had calculated the required uplift of fuel and tasked his co-pilot with supervising the fuelling process.

When Geoff was ready he filed the flight plan by handing it to the airport official who would then send it by Teleprinter, using the Airline Flight Transmission Network (AFTN), to all the other control centres along the route and to the final destination airport, Exeter. As a flight progresses it is monitored and to various degrees controlled by a Flight Information Region (FIR) controller. Geoff also handed in the necessary customs declaration of what was on the aircraft and a list of passengers. Copies of these documents would also have been taken on board Garby by the captain. Exeter were expecting the flight QA 7815 to arrive at around 2045 their time (BST). All this was perfectly normal procedure.

This is what Geoff Whittaker would already have done, not forgetting adjustments for altitude and weather, particularly headwinds, before he told Bill Hickock to load 2,720 litres. Impressed? I am. So if all that was allowed for and the calculations were correct, how come Garby runs out of fuel seven and a half miles before Exeter? Good question.

The AAIB report states that there were 3,178 litres on board at the end of the flight down to Santander. The flight home required 5,902 litres and the outstanding balance is 2,724 litres; hence the request for the upload to be 2,720 litres. We can forget about the odd 4 litres as insignificant. By the way, the other interesting fact available there is that Garby was using about 1,844 litres an hour, 30.73 litres a minute, during the 129 minute flight. If you want to calculate some more allow about three minutes further flying time to Exeter, five minutes taxiing and your eight minutes times 30.73 litres a minute comes to 245.87 litres and that would have brought her home and dry.

While you have your calculator out, have a go at how much fuel did Garby probably actually need for the full 129 minute flight home. The answer is in Chapter 6 to save you the trouble but the bottom line is – according to the captain's calculations – there was plenty of fuel on board for the flight. And so there should have been.

So what did go wrong with the fuelling? Officially we don't know because the AAIB does not tell us but you can read Geoff Whittaker's heartfelt comment in the next chapter and some observations and comments in Chapter 6.

It is also worth bearing in mind an apparently minor

2.1: Flight Plan for flight QA 7815 (G-ARBY)
(Reconstruction; John Allison)

point about the layout of instruments on Garby's flight deck. Pilots often refer to the big 'T'. These are the flight instruments that give both pilots all the vitally important information necessary about the plane's attitude, speed, course, altitude and rate of climb. These instruments are repeated in both pilot positions. The fuel gauges are not part of the big 'T' but are usually placed between the two pilots so that they can be easily seen from either seat. On this Viscount the fuel gauges were only provided in front of the co-pilot in the right-hand seat position.

As well as loading fresh fuel, bowsers could also remove unwanted fuel as might be the case if the aircraft became unserviceable after it had been fuelled. It is not uncommon for an aircraft sitting at a gate ready to be pushed back and depart, to suddenly go unserviceable for a technical reason like a computer failure or landing gear fault. It is full of passengers and fuel and going nowhere. The passengers are taken off to await a replacement aircraft and the original aircraft is taken away for repair work. The airline may need to de-fuel the aircraft at considerable cost of course, for safety reasons. The point here is that such a de-fuelling would not be done by the airport's bowsers but by a special bowser dedicated for that purpose and operated by a maintenance company or the airline. So as an example, at Exeter the Airport Authority's own bowsers would load fuel but never unload it.

A maintenance company, like FlyBe's own, has its own bowser that is able to unload the fuel. Therefore at Exeter and at any other UK airfields only totally 'clean' fuel can be loaded into an aircraft. Furthermore, if fuel is loaded it would never be transferred to another aircraft as such fuel would be considered 'dirty'. Dirty fuel would normally be disposed of safely – and expensively – but it could possibly be used under a special license for some other purpose, like heating the airport buildings. However this would attract all sorts of tax issues and is consequently rarely done.

There is also always a risk of water getting into the fuel tanks and planes do not fly well on water or, indeed, fresh air. This potentially catastrophic situation is strictly guarded against. Regulations were possibly not quite as strict in Spain and whilst the AAIB does not suggest that Garby's fuel was contaminated it does state that the meter reading on the bowser could not have 'reflected the quantity of fuel delivered'. Oh really!

As both the pilots knew of Garby's little weakness in the fuel gauge department, it would have been reasonable to do a physical check of the fuel in the tanks, or rather bladders as that is what you would find if you had a look inside the outer skin of the wings. To facilitate this check 'dripsticks' are provided for all the fuel bladders and there are access panels for these, seemingly all over the underside of the wings.

Most people are familiar with the 'dipstick' in their car engine and a 'dripstick' (Fig. 1) is just an upside down version of this and works with a bit of gravitational assistance. A small hollow tube is fitted and sealed inside the bottom of the fuel bladder and accessed through a flap in the underside of the wing. When this tube is slowly pulled down, with the fuel around it, as the surface of the fuel is reached the liquid will overflow into the tube and run out at the bottom. Neat idea don't you think? The length of the tube inside the fuel at this point is read off against a marker on the wing and the amount of fuel in the bag can be calculated. Simple and reliable but also mucky and smelly as the fuel is now probably dripping down the checker's shirt sleeve and onto the tarmac, and ground crews don't like fuel on the loose and neither do the fire people!

A pilot who does this has then got to go and clean up or flies the plane smelling like a fuel can in your garage. Neither pilot did this simple test, nor did the Alidair company operations manual require them to do so, and the reality was that Garby was about to take off with insufficient fuel for the flight home. For the two-hour and nine minute flight the formal calculations gave a requirement of 3,375 litres with a reserve of 2,527 litres. We don't know how much fuel was on board but it wasn't enough.

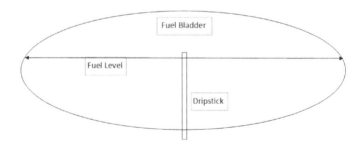

Fig. 1: A 'dripstick' indicates the quantity of fuel in a tank/bladder by allowing the fuel to 'overflow' into a delivery tube which can be measured against a scale.

Heading home

Shortly after a quarter past seven, Sue and Sandra were watching the baggage and cabin catering box being loaded and then started ushering the fifty-eight passengers through the departure gate. It was a short walk to Garby, parked as she was close to the terminal. What would the passengers have made of the fact that the *Armorique* had already sailed out of her berth at the quayside and was now heading north to Plymouth?

The first passenger to make his way to the aircraft kept himself to himself, his coat over his arm and his hat on his head, protecting him from the glaring sun. All this disruption was a considerable inconvenience to him and he looked down at his feet as he walked briskly to the aircraft. All he wanted to do was to get back to his home in Toronto, Canada as quickly as possible.

Behind him came the other fifty-seven passengers and Sue, standing at the forward steps, checked them all on board. The manifest showed that there were a total of nineteen male adults; twenty-four female adults – many of them Spanish domestics, who were probably heading for the UK south coast holiday areas as this week marked the start of the school holidays and there was plenty of work to be had in the south of England. One of the female passengers was heavily pregnant. As well as the adults there were a total of thirteen children and two tiny babies.

Next in line to board after the man from Canada were two young children and their parents. The family had been forced by the circumstances of the ferry failure to leave their caravan behind in Santander but the children were excited to be flying home.

The boy was interested in everything to do with the aircraft and pestered his dad with a string of questions about the wheels, the wings and the engine pods.

'Anyway what is a turbine, Dad?'

'Let's just get on, son. Sometimes the pilot invites a passenger or two to go on the flight deck and see what happens. You may be lucky.'

'Ask him, Dad. Please.'

Dad was actually as interested as his young son but Mum felt that she would have preferred to be safely on the ferry. The Brittany Ferries' staff had promised the family that their caravan would be on the next ferry. That was a bit of an optimistic promise but it satisfied the customers for now. Mrs Maria Quindimil and her husband were returning eventually to Darlington where they worked.

Mrs Patricia Meller from Orpington was returning home from a holiday in Spain with her husband and daughter, Siobhan. Most of the seats on Garby would be full and two seats at the back were, as usual, kept for the two stewardesses; although this job in 1980 was usually done by women it was not uncommon for a man to be trotting up and down the aisle catering for the passengers' needs. Interestingly one major airline, QANTAS, only used male cabin attendants.

The rows of seats were numbered 1 to 13 from the front and each row, up to row 13, had five seats, three on the left of the aisle facing forwards, lettered A to C and the other two, E and F, on the right. (Apx 4.) D was the aisle in this configuration. Row 13 had only two seats in the A and B positions on the left-hand side of the cabin adjacent to the rear door. The two infants, by the way, were carried in the arms of their parents. No overhead lockers for hand baggage were provided as there was no hand baggage and the nets were used for hats and coats. This all seems a bit quaint now, thirty-eight years after the flight.

A larger than life, and well rounded, American couple struggled up the steps and breathlessly squeezed themselves into the starboard window seats in row 2 (Apx 4). The caravan family had four seats across row 4. Two elderly sisters from Scunthorpe were behind the wing on the port side, in row 10, and behind them and almost at the back, in row 11, were the girl from the office, still wearing her new shoes, and her admiring boyfriend. The Bean family of five members were sat in row 2. These seating arrangements are significant because later in the flight they may well have affected their chances of surviving a crash. They certainly did affect their view out of their nearby large, elliptical windows. Interestingly, on this aircraft each window was capable of becoming an emergency exit but none were to be used as such on this flight.

On the flight deck Bill, the co-pilot, called the pre-engine start checks and Geoff responded as he checked the settings of the levers, switches and dials. It is usual for the 'not handling pilot' to call the checks and the 'pilot handling' responds. The complete sequence of checks is: pre-engine start, taxi, pre-take off, after take off, cruise, pre-descent, approach and final. The co-pilot sets all the fuel flow meters to 'zero' and the unit of measurement in Garby was probably made to show pounds (lbs), but it may have shown gallons. These four instruments, one for each engine, were of particular interest because they showed how much fuel had been consumed as the flight progressed. With the fuel gauges unreliable these were the best alternatives for checking the amount of fuel they had left but that depended of course on accurately knowing how much they had on board before starting the engines. Consequently the flight was flawed before it left the ground.

Geoff asked the Control Tower for taxi clearance and set the prop blades to 'ground fine pitch' to avoid overheating the engines; for the actual take off the blades were re-set to 'flight fine'. The propeller movement range for in flight use was from 'flight fine' for take off to 'coarse' for cruising.

Interestingly, assuming you are interested in these 'fine' points of flying a Viscount, there are no mixture controls on a turboprop – the power levers are connected to the Propeller Control Unit (PCU) and Fuel Control Units (FCUs).

Everything is automatic and there are various mechanical and electrical interlocks that control blade pitch and fuel flow to achieve the power required. In flight the fuel flow can be adjusted by 'fuel trimmer' switches and the pilot monitored engine torque and turbine temperature gauges and used these trimmers for fine adjustment.

A couple of minutes later, nicely lined up on Runway 29, Geoff requested clearance to take off. By the way, after landing the 'flight fine' setting was still too coarse for ground manoeuvring and if sufficient power had been applied to make the aircraft taxi it would have over-fuelled and run hot – like trying to drive your car at 10 mph in fifth gear, so the 'ground fine' was pulled – this unlocked the propellers' fine pitch stop and allowed the blade to come back to a finer angle. This was no longer a concern to Garby as she had, strictly speaking, already made her last controlled landing.

As Garby's speed reached take off velocity at around 110 knots (kts) Geoff eased back on the yoke and waited for the nose wheel to lift off the tarmac. It was 1933 local time and Flight QA 7815 was in the air. The after take off check was completed and they were soon climbing easily into the clear blue sky. The Santander departure controller handed the flight over to the first of the FIR (Flight Information Region) controllers who were expecting the flight to pass through their area and come under their control. As soon as it was out of Santander airspace Garby was handed over to the Madrid FIR controller followed by Bordeaux.

A turn to the right of 115 degrees set them on a north-easterly course of around 045 degrees that would initially take them out over the south-east corner of the Bay of Biscay and then over the French coast near Arcachon heading for the Cognac Beacon. West of Bordeaux they would turn left to head north (330 degrees) and join the A25 airway towards Nantes, Dinard and eventually passing to the west of the Channel Islands and heading towards Berry Head, near Brixham in Devon.

In their seats in row ten, behind the wing on the left of the cabin, the taller of the two elderly ladies from Scunthorpe bent over her sister and said, 'Oh do look at how green the sea is, and those little boats look just like ducks in the bath.'

'What nonsense you do talk,' her sister replied, 'and do stop leaning over me. Can't you see you are tipping the plane up?' They looked at each other in disbelief. They had not done much flying.

The 'caravan children' in row four were very excited about the whole adventure and Dad was telling his ten-year-old son how the wings generated the lift force, but the boy was much more interested in watching the wing flexing and bending and thinking it might soon break off – how near the truth he was.

The Dart engines were all working perfectly, their curious deep sigh just about audible in the insulated and pressurized cabin. Sue and Sandra moved up and down the aisle serving drinks and snacks to those who wanted them.

The corpulent Americans accepted drinks and a packet of nuts each from Sandra whilst the Canadian declined the refreshment offer and turned to look out of his window at the green sea far below. He wiped a drop of perspiration off his brow and a little condensation from the window and thought to himself that the windows, all marked 'Emergency Exit', seemed unnecessarily large. *You could pass a body through that*, he thought, and was quite right.

In row 11, at the back of the cabin on the port side, the boyfriend glanced affectionately at the current love of his life, gave her hand a squeeze and felt pleased that today she was relaxed and happy. Her green eyes were gazing down at the little waves that she thought looked like the undulations she saw in the new quilt her grandmother had given her for the large bed in her flat. A bed she hoped eventually to share with her disarming young man. He sipped his drink, oblivious to her thoughts.

In the cockpit, Geoffrey settled the heading down on to 022 and adjusted the power levers to produce a speed over the ground of around 270 kts. Speeds in aircraft are always stated in knots as this equates to the nautical miles scale on charts and makes navigation simpler. Before this was standardised, particularly in the age of the Dakota, accidents and navigation errors occurred due to pilots thinking in 'kts' and using 'mph'. This was particularly dangerous when slowing for final approach or taking off heavy on a hot, windless day.

In 1980 the pilots may have chosen to hand fly the aircraft as there was no requirement for a serviceable autopilot because there were two pilots on the flight deck. We do not know whether Garby had autopilot or not. Autopilots had been available since WWII but compared to the more modern units they were quite crude and some were merely wing levellers controlled by a simple gyroscope. The best help a pilot had without an autopilot were, and still are, the manual trimmers. These enable the aircraft to be balanced in all axes – nose to tail and wing tip to wing tip – and also directionally in the case of the rudder trim – for the speed set on the throttles and delivered by the engines.

Unless turbulence, weight distribution or pressure changes caused an imbalance then the plane would fly along straight and level as it had been set up to do. The pilot did have to make slight trim changes as the fuel was burnt up, or even if a passenger moved around in the cabin. It would also have been necessary to re-trim if fuel was transferred from one tank to another. The pilot did not have to be straining on the yoke for example to keep the nose up but he did have to keep at least one hand on the yoke. Today computers and the autopilot take care of all that and all the pilot has to do is make occasional adjustments, drink his coffee and be ready to take control if necessary.

This sector from Santander to Exeter was about 540 miles and the estimated flying time a few minutes over two hours. They were at Flight Level (FL) 18, that is 18,000 feet, and were now under the control of the FIR at Brest. To have flown higher, ideally at 24,000 feet where the air was thinner, would have burnt less fuel when they reached that altitude, but climbing up there required more fuel than would have been saved. The little snag with FL 24 is that it is also the altitude at which the pressure differential between inside and outside the aircraft is at its greatest.

There may also have been concerns about the integrity of the hull to take pressurization due to the age of the aircraft and this factor was the major influence in the choice of the flight level. The higher the aircraft flew the greater the risk of cabin pressure differential causing a rapid decompression. How safe were those large old oval windows in those frames? No one in the industry was ever likely to forget the disastrous instant depressurisation in the Comets when, in 1954, two of them crashed partly due to hairline cracks caused by metal fatigue near some windows and aerials. The original windows were square and this fact contributed to failure. As the cabins exploded all on board both planes were killed.

Flight Deck visitors

Soon after 1900 (BST) Sandra asked Sue if she thought this would be a good time for those passengers who would like to do so to visit the flight deck. Sue agreed and went forward to ask Geoff if he would be willing to have visitors. Whilst this is not usual practise now, mainly for security reasons, in 1980 it was common as it had been for many years previously. It was a great thrill I remember to stand behind the pilot's seat of a 707 in the late 1960s on a flight back to the UK from North America, looking out of the flight deck windows to see light, fluffy cotton wool clouds floating over a dark green sea and the soft glow of an orange sun just about to rise over the eastern horizon.

The Americans declined Sandra's invitation with a 'we are comfortable here thank you'. But the caravan 'boys' were falling over themselves to be the first to stand behind Geoff. 'Do not touch anything !' 'No Dad. I won't.'

Geoff mechanically explained how the main controls worked and how he kept Garby heading in the right direction. He carefully avoided any mention of the fuel gauges up to the point when the ten-year-old asked how much fuel was needed for the flight.

'Lots,' sniffed Geoff. 'Shall we give someone else a visit now young man?'

Two by two about half the passengers chose to visit the cockpit over the next hour or so and this gave cause for comment in the subsequent investigation. (Note 2.1.)

All was apparently going smoothly and Geoff was just left with the little concern about the fuel gauges. Garby showed her age more in the cockpit than anywhere else on board. The leather seat coverings were worn to holes in places, black paint had been rubbed away on corners of instrument cases, hand grips on the yokes and throttles were all tired and threadbare and there was a general air of decay; a couple of flies occasionally did an orbit of the instruments in a hopeless attempt to escape to the fresh air outside. Bill was smoking, Geoff was coughing; it was a cosy, warm but unhealthy atmosphere. They crossed the French coast above a long beach and those in the right-hand window seats had a fine view of the green-rich farmland near the little town of Arachon.

Geoffrey

Geoffrey Whittaker was born into a middle class family in Blackburn in 1926. When he was seven the family moved to Jersey and Geoffrey had a happy childhood enjoying all that the pre-war Channel Islands had to offer a young lad: sea paddling, sand castle building, cream-rich milk, abundant tomatoes, 'Royal' potatoes and importantly plenty of air, much fresher than that available in the industrial Midlands. His dad had a lung condition and now the family were content in their new environment. Geoffrey proved to be a bright and determined lad and after his eleventh birthday in 1937 he went off to the local grammar school, Victoria College. All was well until World War II and German bombers arrived on 28th June 1940 killing forty-four islanders and wrecking a lorry full of tomatoes on a Guernsey harbour wall. Fortunately all of the Channel Island schools had been evacuated to the English mainland the week before and Geoffrey and his school chums, together with a lot of school equipment and teachers, had been packed off to Oxford.

He joined the Oxford Air Cadets as soon as he was old enough to do so and began to learn quickly all that he could about aviation. He wanted to be 'up there'. It is not difficult to imagine how the chance of early responsibility, excitement, comradeship and 'flying his dream' would lead a young man to ignore the appalling risks he faced. He was sixteen and he wanted to take on Hitler. His mother must have wept and wept. He was soon off to Canada to train as a pilot and became one of the latter heroes of the end game of the RAF's battle against the Luftwaffe. He took part as a Flight Lieutenant, piloting his own Dakota in raids and parachute operations, as well as the Berlin Airlift, and at the end of the war, the repatriation of Allied Prisoners of War from Japan. None of this was of course in his mind as he flew north in this tired, old, clapped-out Viscount with tired old Bill Hickock sitting to his right, alternately looking down on the fields of France and then scanning again the fuel gauges. 'Aviate, navigate, communicate.' He thought of the airman's trusted adage and at 1946 they passed over Nantes, France.

More Flight Deck unease

At approximately 2010 (BST) they were in the area of Dinard, northern France, and expected the flight to be handed over to London FIR. Suddenly, and without warning, one of the port fuel gauge indicators fell to zero and then flipped over to read 'full'. This occurrence was repeated on another gauge and various other instrument fluctuations occurred. The starboard gauge showed a reading indicating that they had 500 litres on that side and that the amount was reducing steadily, as expected, by a little more than thirty litres a minute. Both pilots were uneasy but this was Garby's usual behaviour.

As they passed over the Channel Islands the flight was handed over from Brest FIR to the Channel Islands' control zone. The Channel Islands have a special control zone within London FIR because of the heavy amount of traffic they experience. Soon they were passed to London FIR by Jersey as they approached Skerry – that is aircraft speak for 50 degrees north latitude. Both pilots clearly heard the handover to London come through on their headsets:

'Golf Bravo Yankee, you are leaving Brest airspace. Contact London Information on 118.475 – they have your details."

The FIR controller's assistant would have talked to the next FIR on the telephone line prior to the handover and passed on all the relevant information; hence the, 'they have your details', as part of the transmission. Geoff acknowledged and then called London:

'London, good evening. Golf Bravo Yankee, maintaining flight level one eight. Checked Skerry at 2017. Estimating Berry Head at 2030 BST."

When making contact the captain would confirm his flight level, hence – 'maintaining flight level one eight' – and give his time estimate for the next waypoint – this allows the controller to check for any possible conflicting traffic and confirm that the flight is going according to plan.

London picked up the flight as expected and Geoff made the left turn to the north-west on 332 as Bill re-tuned the 'Nav' radios and soon they were heading for the Berry Head VOR beacon with around 140 miles to fly. This course was to take them about ten miles west of Jersey and after that just west of the south-western corner of Guernsey. This was one of the several course changes Geoff had to make to follow the airway. Provided the pilot sticks to all the rules and follows all the correct procedures everything works well, but whenever there is a human hand involved things can, and indeed do, go wrong (Apx 8).

Geoff looked down at Jersey and thought of Shirley, his wife, at home at Pont Rose Farm (Fix 6.5), not a quarter of a mile from the main passenger entrance to the airport; the noise of aircraft coming and going a constant backdrop to her life. She would soon be taking the dogs out for their evening romp around the farm's big field. Geoff was pleased that he would be home tomorrow for the weekend. He had booked to tee off at the golf course at ten o'clock on Saturday morning and was looking forward to a pint and lunch with friends after the round. Geoff liked to win but coped perfectly well with losing and his losing was frequently caused by lack of concentration when a plane flew over.

'The game's the thing,' he would say and an opponent would reply with a chuckled, 'Really? I thought the plane was the thing!'

Shirley, the dogs and a round of golf were the main pleasures in his life when he was not flying. He was lucky that he did a job he loved, but this week he was really looking forward to a couple of days off.

Not surprisingly, as there were still passengers on the flight deck, Geoff did not feel it appropriate to say to Bill what he was turning over in his mind… *Do you think we should go into Jersey and top up the tanks?*

Instead he lifted himself up in his seat, looked meaningfully at Bill, then at the fuel gauges, then out of Bill's window and down at Jersey. Bill curled a lip and gave an almost imperceptible shake of his head.

'No way,' he mouthed.

It was one of those finely balanced ideas with just a few more 'againsts' than 'fors', and because of the flight deck visitors the pilots did not have a full discussion and then the moment had passed. It was better and certainly cheaper to continue.

The downside of landing at Jersey or Guernsey would have been a delay of at least forty-five minutes. Landing fees alone would have been at least £500. The plane would have landed at around 1915 and that would have been outside normal hours. Out of hours staffing is paid by the hour at a higher rate and ground crew, control staff as well as airport management and security costs would have set Alidair back more than £1,200, money that they could ill afford to lose. At Exeter the scheduled arrival would have been more than an hour late and that would have also incurred more costs. Safety does indeed come at a price. They flew on.

The generally accepted best practise among aircrew flying into Exeter from the continent was that all visitors

44

had to be clear of the flight deck by the time that the flight passed through 50 degrees north latitude (Skerry). At this point the pilot was expecting a change of course and height instruction from the controller at Exeter Approach and there was serious work to be done in the cockpit as the crew prepared for landing. Garby now had about forty-three miles still to fly and was around fifteen miles from Berry Head and thirty-five miles from Exeter Airport. We do not know when the final visitor to the flight deck went back to the cabin but later the AAIB report was critical of passengers being on the flight deck when important decisions had to be made. At 2028, near Berry Head, Garby turned right onto a direct track towards the Exeter directional beacon and was cleared to descend to 4,000 feet (FL4).

I need to give a quick health warning here concerning the amount of technical flying issues coming up in the next two paragraphs – some will find them interesting and others won't. Personally I like to know how it all works and I am very grateful to my helpers (particularly the stalwart John Allison) for the contributions. So do feel free to hop along to the last paragraphs of this chapter if you are not up for a technical briefing. You have been warned!

G-ARBY would probably have had a very basic transponder that allowed it to be seen outside the primary radar range by the Secondary Surveillance System (SSS). In 1980 Exeter Radar did not have the ability to pick up SSS transmissions and could only 'see' an aircraft electronically at relatively short range – maybe twenty miles, or less, south of Berry Head. So Garby would have been cleared down to the safe level for obstacle clearance of FL4 (4,000 feet).

The minimum sector safe altitude in the Exeter Western quadrant area is 3,400 feet and Garby would have been held above that level until Exeter Radar identified the flight and allowed further descent. Garby would then have been let down in stages until she was at around 2,000-2,500 feet and then vectored (given instructions on where to go) onto the ILS (Instrument Landing System). When the plane was fully established on the Localiser and Glideslope beams it would descend on the 3.5 degree glide path into Exeter. This procedure would have resulted in Garby being at around 2,000 feet as it approached Ottery St Mary and that is where we find her at the beginning of the next chapter.

ATC at Exeter came through on the radio at 2028 when the aircraft was approaching Berry Head, near Brixham, and cleared Garby for descent. Exeter could track her on radar from this point. A turn to the right may well have been authorised when the flight was about fifteen miles southeast of Berry Head, effectively giving the pilot a shortcut to the Branscombe area. A few minutes later they were cleared down to Flight Level 4 and given clearance for a direct track to the Exeter Non Directional Beacon (NDB) that transmitted 'EX' in morse code. Effectively this meant that whilst their navigation target or waypoint was Berry Head they were cleared to take a short cut route and make an early right turn. This is usual practise in this situation as the lower airspace was not busy.

We know that Geoff did indeed turn right but we do not know exactly where he crossed the coast as there is no record of this, although the controller at Exeter would have been watching the radar trace. However we do know where witnesses saw Garby about fifteen minutes later. That position suggests that Garby was following the normal route and crossed the coast close to Branscombe, less than a mile west of Beer Head. Height was reducing now and was probably below 3,000 feet.

On the flight deck the pilots were running the pre-landing checks and Geoff was adjusting speed and trim. Bill was turning on landing lights and was ready to lower the undercarriage and bring in probably ten degrees of flap. The flaps give the aircraft more lift at a slower speed. Their speed now was down to around 120 kts as they flew on over the rolling Devon fields and approached, at 2,000 feet, East Hill to the east of Ottery St Mary. They were nearly home and dry – well not quite home, but certainly dry.

1.5: Fuel gauges, Viscount V701 G-ALWF, at Duxford.
(Picture; Jim Rider 2014)

3

Going down

All engines stopped / Silence in the cabin / Doctor's family to the rescue / Going in/ Nothing she could do/ Poor girl/ Barely in control / Charles runs on/ 'Sunshine' in the meadow / Final seconds in the air / Down with a bang / Blood in the field / She comes to rest

All engines stopped

'*Mayday. Mayday. Mayday,*' said Whittaker after the engines had stopped over East Hill.

'*Golf Alpha Romeo Bravo Yankee. One point fiver miles east, Ottery St Mary heading to join Exeter two seven final. All engines stopped. Suspect fuel exhausted. Turning south to make forced landing. All stations. Mayday.*'

The call clearly sent was immediately received at Exeter Airport and the flight controller managing Garby's progress extended his left hand a few inches and pressed the red alarm button in front of him. Lights flashed and a bell rang in the

Exeter Area control room of the Devon Fire Brigade at Clyst St George, three and a half miles south-west of the airfield.

Co-pilot Hickock, now wide awake, looked at Whittaker and saw him move his hand away from the landing gear control that he had been about to lower.

'You can do it Geoff – wheels up will be best.'

'Yes,' said Geoff. 'Wheels up, nose up. All signs on. Feathering all props. Flaps ten set. Tell the girls to check all the belts and prepare for brace.'

Bill clicked the signs on and then spoke calmly on the cabin PA. 'Ladies and gentleman, this is the co-pilot. We are about to make an emergency landing. Make sure you are strapped in to your seats and be ready to adopt the brace position when I tell you. Cabin staff, check the passengers and then take your seats. Please do not be alarmed and remain calm. This is a routine procedure.'

Like hell it is, he thought.

Whittaker was scanning the fields to his left, looking for somewhere that might possibly serve as a landing field. He had walked beside the River Otter a number of times but never thought he would have to do the almost impossible task of landing a Viscount there. Airliners did not land in fields, they landed at airports. He pushed the stick forward a bit and, against all his instincts to maintain his height, he knew he had to lose most of the 1,800 feet he had under him if he was going to get her onto the ground. He was also going much too fast.

Retired Master Mariner Alan Nicholl and his wife Jan were sitting in their lounge at the back of their comfortable home in Slade Close, Ottery St Mary. (Fix 3.0.) The patio door was wide open and suddenly they heard what sounded like, in their words, 'a car back-firing; a sort of coughing'. They quickly went outside and saw a big plane flying low. It was directly over a mature oak tree in the garden and thirty-eight years later they are still very sure of its position and height.

As they watched three propellers were feathering and slowing down, and then the fourth engine cut out. They were used to seeing planes flying to the north of the house on their way to Exeter, but never one gliding in this position to their south. They agreed that something was badly wrong; obviously a serious incident was in progress.

The large American woman, in the starboard window seat in row 2, was beginning to feel a little uneasy. She was aware that something had changed but was not quite sure what. Her husband beside her was still asleep. Behind she heard a baby crying.

Sue the stewardess ran down the aisle and into the cockpit. A few seconds later she came out, her face ashen as if she had seen a ghost. She ran back calling, 'Seat belts please everyone. Put your seat belts on quickly.'

The American woman saw that the propellers were winding down and turning slowly in the wind. Below to the right, she could see houses and a large church on a hill. Something was wrong. She poked her husband in the ribs.

Sue called, 'There is nothing to worry about', but she sounded as if there was.

Now, a glider, Garby was progressing along the length of Longdog's Lane on the south side of Ottery St Mary. This lane runs just about east to west and Peter Harris lived at the eastern end, at the junction with Grandisson Drive. (Fix 3.1.) From here he had a clear view of the sky in front of his house and away to East Hill to his left as he faced to the south.

Peter was in the front garden of his house when Garby approached from East Hill and flew clearly into his view. As it passed him it turned slightly to the right, and appeared to follow the line of the lane, putting the plane on a course close to due west. All the time it was descending and three of the engines were feathering and in his words 'making a sound like lawnmowers.'

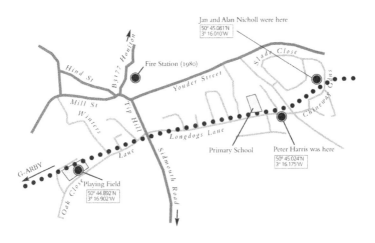

Fig. 2: G-ARBY's route from the east of Ottery St Mary along Longdog's Lane. (All diagrams by Chris Wakefield unless otherwise marked.)

They were in fact just slowing down as the power had been cut by the lack of fuel. He judged the aircraft to be at about half the usual height for aircraft approaching Exeter.

Something is definitely wrong with that one. Might be some sort of exercise, he thought.

Then he set off for fields down by the river as that was where he judged the plane was heading.

In the playing field, further to the west in Clapp's Lane, (Fix 3.2) his little niece, Lucy, was playing with her friends. They saw the plane and it frightened them. It was 'making a funny noise and it was too low.'

The girls ran screaming, as little girls often do, to hide in the bushes but after a minute, when the noise had stopped, they came out again and carried on playing.

A mile and a half west of East Hill now and Geoff had broken into a cold sweat, his hands clammy on the controls, his back straining against the old leather seat. He was thinking faster than he had ever thought in his life because he knew more than anyone else on board that he was probably going to die in the next few minutes. He wiped the back of his hand across his lips. Survival odds were slim – much too slim.

He was pressing her nose down – at 600 feet now they were still too high – he must lose more height but keep enough so that he could maintain airspeed in case Lady Luck smiled on him at the last moment and he could make for a reasonable landing spot. Bill snapped out one word and it captured perfectly the situation they were in and how he felt about it.

Silence in the cabin

Inside the plane there was almost silence; a strange, un-natural calm. There was no sound to be heard from the feathering engines and only a barely perceptible light whistle broke the deceptive peace as Garby glided along. There was no vibration, no shouting out, only the sound of a baby crying at the back of the cabin.

The father of the two young children peered intently at the two feathering engines on the port wing. In row 4 he was right beside them and his young son was sitting beside him. The man knew that there was something badly wrong and had worked out that it must be a fuel issue or some sort of electrical failure as none of the engines were firing. He looked anxiously across the aisle to his wife, and beside her his much loved little daughter.

He kept his racing thoughts to himself – *They can't land like this*, he supposed. *Oh my god – my family, my children!*

He shook his head and gestured to his wife to tighten the girl's seat belt. Mum's jaw dropped and her eyes widened. She felt a deep panic creeping over her. She pulled on her daughter's seat belt and then her own as the plane tilted over to the left. In row 2 Michael Bean turned in his seat to see if his wife was alright; she was white-faced and staring at him, her eyes very large.

Now someone behind her called out, 'What's happening? There's something wrong with the plane.'

There was indeed.

On his left the River Otter snaked away towards the

south and Geoff saw that there was a long, level field beside it, to the west. That was his best option and he quickly made his mental plan for bringing her in there. Exeter Control came back on his com radio…

'Exeter Approach. Alidair Bravo Yankee, your Mayday received. All services alerted and standing by. Please confirm total persons on board as sixty-two. Good luck.'

Hickock replied to this with a brief, 'Affirmative; sixty-two souls.'

Bill was very aware that he could do nothing to help except leave Geoff to fully concentrate on the impossible task he was attempting. He knew that if anyone could actually do the impossible it was Geoff Whittaker. Geoff felt the controls becoming heavier and less responsive as the airspeed decreased. He had to balance all the natural forces affecting the flight – raising the nose maintained height and slowed the aircraft but less speed meant less lift and less response. He could not risk a stall but he was still well above the stalling speed of 97 mph (84 kts).

Garby crossed the River Otter banking left, and around 170 yards south of the town bridge Geoff tightened the turn. Her speed was down now to close on 150 mph (130 kts). She was descending steeply through 400 feet and heading for the Salston Manor Hotel (Fix 3.3), less than half a mile ahead of her to the south. Over the cricket field her wheels were up, ten degrees of flap were down.

Below his window to the left was the wooded, disused railway track and he could clearly see walkers with their dogs looking up at him and pointing. He envied them. Seconds later Garby cleared the tall, elegant hotel chimneys by less

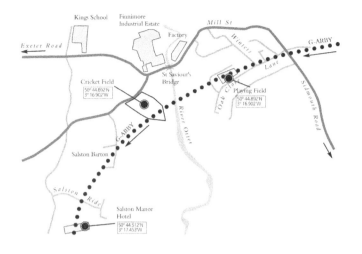

Fig. 3: G-ARBY flight path over Ottery St Mary.
(Oak Close to Salston Manor Hotel)

than a hundred feet and the pilot technically committed a criminal offence. He was fortunate on two counts however; firstly there was no officer of the law around to arrest him and secondly the ground beyond the hotel to the south sloped downhill.

Hotel guests, their evening dinner over, were enjoying each other's company and taking drinks in the garden. They heard a curious lawnmower, like sound from above and looked up.

Doctor's family to the rescue

At ten to nine in the Bradshaw-Smith family home (Fix 3.4), a pleasant dormer bungalow lying about sixty metres to the south-west of the Salston Manor Hotel, most of the family had finished their evening meal in the dining room at the front of the house and had begun to tidy the plates away to the kitchen. The family comprised Doctor Jeremy Bradshaw-Smith, his wife Ann, daughter Emma, aged nineteen, Charles and his younger brother Robert aged fifteen.

Charles Bradshaw-Smith was an athletic young man of eighteen years and as he had been playing cricket for most of the evening he had arrived home too late to join the family meal at the dining table. He was taking his dinner on a tray through to his favourite room, the lounge at the back of the house. This room had a glorious, southerly view through large French doors that led onto a small patio. Beyond, over gently sloping fields and woods in the far distance, the River Otter often sparkled in the afternoon sunshine. The family dog, Betsy, regarded Charles as his 'pet person', as Charles would often sneak her food scraps when Mum was not looking.

Amongst his other sporting achievements, Charles was able to list several area titles in Devon County races. He was a keen member of Exeter Harriers, and was able to run the 800 metres in under two minutes – provided that he was in the right kit and on a running track. Now, in 1980, he had just finished his first year at London University and was in training for the second London Marathon in which he was planning to run the following year. His high fitness level was about to prove useful.

His older sister, Emma, was standing in the lounge looking out through the patio door to the green lush fields and wood beyond. As she looked to the south she saw that some breaks were appearing in the grey clouds and wondered if tomorrow might turn out to be a better day.

Suddenly, to her astonishment, Emma found herself looking at a low flying white airliner. It had come into view from her left and must have only just cleared the tall chimneys on the top of the Salston Hotel. It appeared to be around a hundred metres away and was gliding quickly south towards the edge of the wood she knew as the Alder Grove. (Fix 3.5.) She could not hear any engine noise but there was a sort of whistling sound coming from the plane. She stared at the airliner, her hand at her mouth.

'Oh my god… Dad!' she shouted. 'Dad… Charles… it's a plane, quick! It can't land,' she thought, 'the wheels aren't down.'

Charles rushed in carrying his dinner on a tray. He looked out of the window, following Emma's stare and quickly realised the full horror of what he was seeing.

'There's a plane crashing – a big one. Get Dad… ring the police or somebody. I'm going after it.'

Emma opened the French doors and rushed out onto the patio as Charles dropped his dinner down noisily onto the coffee table, breaking a tumbler. Then he set off across the garden, vaulting over the three bar fence and then the electric fence and on into the field beyond. The plane was still in sight and he was chasing after it down through the field. His young brother, Robert, ran after him and tried to keep up.

3.1 above: G-ARBY glides low over the Salston Manor Hotel. 2052
17th July, 1980.

3.2 below: Heading south from the Salston Hotel towards the Alder Grove.
Clearance height verified by witnesses
(Reconstructions by Jim Rider)

Going in

In the air, Geoff straightened up for a few hundred yards and then ahead there was a grove of trees. He banked left to line up on the field that he could now clearly see ahead and added some more flap to quickly slow her. Then he deliberately lost some more height and pulled the nose up … *Still too fast – too fast*, he thought.

He shouted to Bill, 'I'm going in right of that tree on its own… in that gap.'

Bill gasped, 'You're doing it… you're doing fine. Just keep the nose up.' Geoff braced himself back into his seat. He was going in.

When he heard Charles shout to Emma, Doctor Jeremy Bradshaw-Smith came rushing out onto the patio. Doctor Jeremy was one of the local GPs in Ottery St Mary and he had practised at the surgery there for many years. As he ran out to Emma he saw the plane travelling fast and passing down the west side of the Alder Grove and then begin a slow turn to the left, as if the pilot was seeking a clear landing place. Jeremy knew he would not find one in the Alder Grove but just beyond the trees there was a clear field with just a few isolated oaks. This was known as Coronation Meadow. The ground between the house and the far end of the Alder Grove, and the field beyond, slopes down a substantial eighteen metres and Jeremy estimated the speed of the plane at more than a hundred miles an hour, perhaps a 120. It was about ninety feet high but as it passed along it lost some height until he was looking at it horizontally. (Note 3.1.) The crash was imminent. Jeremy quickly instructed Emma to ring the Police and then run down the lane to the gate between the cottages (Fix 3.6) to show the fire and ambulance crews where to turn into the field.

Emma ran to the hall at once and was soon talking to the emergency services on the phone. They knew that there was an incident in progress because the Mayday was being actioned from the flight control centre at Exeter, but until Emma's call came in they had received no details of a crash location. Emma was the first to give these details and with red buttons being hit all over Devon, emergency vehicles were leaving their bases and a large and complex disaster response operation was in progress. However the Ottery St Mary Fire Station had not yet been contacted.

Jeremy had quickly run around to his car at the front of the house where he grabbed his medical bag and a 'giving set' (Note 3.2) and the one pack of plasma that he had at home. Ann, the lady of the house, the dishes forgotten, was following the boys down through the field but she was well behind them.

Ann Bradshaw-Smith was a fully trained and experienced Nightingale Nurse (Note 3.3) and she was mentally preparing herself to do the best that was possible for multiple casualties before the emergency medical teams arrived. Daughter Emma was running down the lane to the bottom gate beyond Devil's Bend so that she could show the ambulances and fire engines where to turn into the field.

Nothing she could do

At the back of the cabin, just in front of the rear door, the girl from the ferry office, in her window seat, turned to face her boyfriend. Ten minutes ago they had been a happy young couple but in the last minute she had become emotional as the awful reality of what was happening to them slowly crept over her. She had never been in a situation like this. Her instinct was always to be in control of what was happening, she felt safe that way, but that was gone now. Nothing she could do. At this moment all she wanted in life was life itself and the good and kindly man sitting beside her.

I am going to die; will it hurt, will it be quick? – her thoughts raced away.

She took his hand in hers and kissed it. His blue eyes were wide, staring at trees and a distant silver river silently sliding past below. Then he looked steadily at her, saying nothing, but his hand was shaking in hers.

At the very back of the cabin, strapping themselves into the two seats to the rear of the door, were Sue and Sandra, the stewardesses. They, with commendable professionalism, reminded themselves of the emergency evacuation drills and assumed that they would live through the crash that they knew was now no more than two minutes away.

Poor girl

Near the front of the cabin, the two children of the family who hoped to see their caravan again had picked up on their mother's anxiety and were becoming louder and more excited in their demands for mum's attention and reassurances. Mum instinctively tried to be calm but her mind was racing ahead through the next few minutes and she could only manage a nervous, 'It will be alright dears. The pilot knows what he is doing.'

But she knew she was fibbing and the little girl in particular is not at all convinced.

Two rows in front of the van family the large American man can contain himself no longer; shaking uncontrollably, and to his wife's profound embarrassment, he wet himself and threw up. She wished the earth would open and swallow her – it was about to do just that.

Barely in control

On the flight deck, Geoff was doing mental cartwheels calculating the best impact velocity. He wanted her speed much lower than the normal touch down velocity of 133 mph (116 kts) and knew she would stall out both wings at 96 mph (83 kts). (Note 3.4.) Somewhere in between is the best option for least damage. He quickly decided that he wanted impact at around 126 mph (109 kts) but he now had very little control of this lumbering, heavy, dying bird. He pulled the nose up to slow her. Ahead and about twenty degrees to port, he could see a level field just beyond a wood, but there were some isolated trees and whilst they appear tiny and insignificant from this distance, he knew that anything hard and substantial directly in the path of a landing airliner will cause catastrophic damage and probably fatalities.

Now he had no choice. He would bring her down there; wheels up so that she would slide. The field is part of

Bishop's Court Farm run by Oliver Carter and Oliver was in for a few surprises.

Geoff banked Garby to the left and then, three seconds later, thirty degrees right to line up on what he hoped would be a clear, straight landing strip, but he had seen that there were isolated trees in the way. He pulled the nose up sharply and lost his view of the ground. Impact was seconds away. A bang, a shudder and a skew to the left; they hit the top of a tall tree on the edge of the Alder Grove. They were going down now; Garby was finally out of air miles. Screams and shouts from the cabin behind shake Geoff –

'Oh my god, this is what it's like. I am out of luck this time!'

Charles runs on

His breathing quickened, his leg muscles tense and warmed, his trainers bouncing lightly over the ruts in the grassy meadow for this was not a running track – Charles was competing in a cross country and the only other competitor was a silent airliner.

Level with his eyes and directly ahead of him, the plane he was pursuing was remarkably maintaining its height but the ground was now dropping away. The only sounds were his breathing and his soft, quick footfall on the dry grass. He was 200 yards now from the house and turned back to see if the others were following, 'It's terrible… terrible. They will all be dead!' But nobody was close enough to hear him. Robert was just in sight, coming into the field.

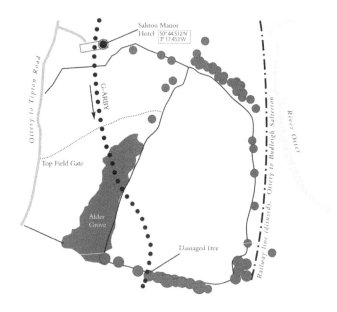

Fig. 4 (above): G-ARBY flight path south of Salston Manor Hotel

Ahead he saw the plane, still in the air, bank to the left and after crossing over the Alder Grove it banked sharply right – the pilot was lining up for a landing.

The aircraft hit a tree with its left wing (Fix 3.7)(Pic 3.3) slicing off the top branches, not quite horizontally, but with the port wing tilting up a few degrees. The impact slewed it left a little but the pilot skilfully managed to straighten up despite damage to the wing. The rudder was intact. It was still flying at just under 100 mph and it weighed around twenty five tonnes, equal to three double decker busses.

3.3: Damage to the top branches of the tree
at the north edge of Coronation Meadow.
(Picture; Jim Rider 2014)

'Sunshine' in the meadow

Edwin Locke was a sprightly thirty-nine-year-old. He was an
able and hard working farmhand who did most of the physical
work at Bishop's Court Farm where he had worked all his life.
He was known to all, far and wide, by the very apt nickname
of 'Sunshine Locke' for indeed he was, and still is at seventy-
four, a happy, warm-hearted and cheerful character. 'The Sun
shines out of his face' some said; others, quite the reverse.

The farm was owned by a Miss Cave and managed for
her by the resourceful and dynamic Oliver Carter, who was
always on the lookout for good business ideas to turn to profit

on the land he leased, hence his interest in the many race horses he trained. He was well known and respected locally. In the field known as Coronation Meadow on Bishop's Court Farm between the lane and the River Otter, were now around 200 sheep, five race horses and a gliding airliner.

Edwin was taking the air in the back garden of the farm cottage in which he lived with his wife, Pam. He was watching the sheep congregating in the 'dimpsey', as they always did as twilight descended. Pam was, at this moment, at her mum's house further down the lane to the south towards Tipton, so she was a bit further away but she clearly saw the drama unfold as did Edwin.

As Garby twisted and turned into view over the Alder Grove, away to their left towards Ottery, Edwin clearly saw the plane clip the top of a tall tree and heard the branches breaking. Garby lurched, then banged down into Carter's field, and slid headlong towards the Lone Oak tree. (Fix 3.8.) Terrified horses galloped away towards the farm buildings, 500 metres to the south. Not surprisingly Edwin's first thoughts were for his sheep. Pam thought the plane which was sliding fast over the field, might turn towards her. Edwin ran towards the Lone Oak and had about 170 metres to cover. He did not notice Charles sprinting in from the Alder Grove on his left.

Final seconds in the air

Sue and Sandra had done all they possibly could for the passengers and had earlier run to their seats at the back of the cabin. Through the door window beside them they could see clear sky for a couple of seconds as Garby banked to the right and then, as she levelled, they saw that they were only a few feet above the treetops. Now they protected themselves by bending over their knees and covered the backs of their necks with their hands. Some passengers were screaming now. The nose of the aircraft suddenly kicked up and they were thrown back in their seats.

Bill Hickock tensed his grip on his co-pilot's seat. He should have gone to the brace position but instinctively felt that if he watched everything happening he was helping Geoff.

They slid over the trees and, as Geoff banked hard right, Bill was thrown against the side of the cockpit, banging his knee painfully. Then a loud bang from the port wing and a twisting wrench to the left, quickly corrected to the right as Geoff again forced the stick hard over to starboard. She was heavy now, too slow to stay in the air. In her final moments the whole of Garby's frame was protesting as Bill called out a string of his favourite words; they seemed to encourage her to stay in the air for a moment, but within two seconds she gave up her brave fight and crashed down onto the back end of her belly and, at ninety miles an hour, charged at the Lone Oak just to her left. Number one prop was torn clean away as it hit the ground and then the oak.

The young couple were desperately clinging to each other and she was burying her face into his neck. She was sobbing uncontrollably and he was still shaking, now violently. Hats and coats flew out of the netting; locker doors banged open at the front of the cabin and the whole plane was shaking and lurching.

3.4: Reconstruction of last moments of Garby's flight.
The + mark is to scale and marks the point of impact.
(Jim Rider)

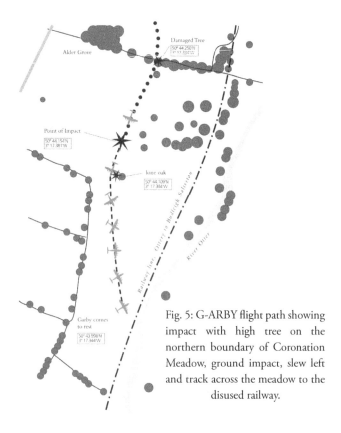

Fig. 5: G-ARBY flight path showing impact with high tree on the northern boundary of Coronation Meadow, ground impact, slew left and track across the meadow to the disused railway.

In front of them, the two elderly sisters, now facing death, were at odds as usual. The elder was the natural leader but now her face was ashen and she was sobbing loudly.

'It's awful, awful… dear sweet Jesus save me.'

The shorter, younger sister, now calmness itself, for no reason that anyone could have fathomed, looked up at her as if she had lost her mind and said, 'It's alright dear. This is how they land at Exeter. We are fine.' And indeed they were – so far.

Below and in front of them, terrified sheep were scattering and expensive race horses snorted and galloped away. Then Garby was finally down, out of the sky and sliding on her belly. She had left her natural element for ever.

Down with a bang

Unseen by Charles, Garby had hit the dry ground with a bang that was heard a mile and a half away in Ottery and across the river in Wiggaton village. She left a slight depression in the ground that is still to be seen. (Pic 3.5) Dust went up. A heavy cloud quickly filled the air and then, within seconds, he heard what sounded like a roaring, big stricken animal fighting for life as metal bumped and scraped along the grassy ground with a terrible scream. He realised that the plane was down in Oliver Carter's field.

Before he had started running down the field, Doctor Jeremy had seen the large dust cloud rising into the air in the distance. He heard the deep boom as the plane hit

3.5: The slight depression clearly shows the slew to the left caused by the impact with the outer part of the port wing and the Lone Oak.
(Picture; Jim Rider 2014)

the ground hard followed by the sounds of it sliding and banging along the grass. Horses whinnied, hooves galloped and most of the 200 sheep bleated pathetically. The time was 2053.

Charles ran on and, despite the physical effort to which he was well accustomed, he was thinking clearly, all his senses on fire, his thoughts racing ahead. He knew he was about to witness sights the likes of which most Devon people had never seen in peacetime. There would be bodies just around the corner of the Alder Grove on this drizzly and grey summer's evening. There would be death and horror. Still he ran, now looking back to see if his father was following.

'Dad I need you here with me. They will need a doctor – hurry!' In Coronation Meadow the plane was on the ground, pounding and rattling along. The pilots gripped their seats, their knuckles white and pulses racing, all control of the aircraft now lost. Could the worst be over or was it still to come? Passengers shouted and screamed and a terrible groaning and banging came from Garby's soft belly as she thundered along, now at more than seventy miles an hour.

The number one engine, the port outer, had been almost but not completely wrenched from its wing mounting pod – probably as Garby hit the ground (Fix 3.9), and blades from other engines went spinning away in any direction. These blades could have torn through the main fuselage, wreaking carnage on the people inside but fortunately they did not and set off instead in search of sheep to dissect.

Still travelling fast the port wing hit the Lone Oak, marking it forever with concentric rings as if it had been drilled (Note 3.5) (Pic 3.6). This brief, forceful impact momentarily stopped the port wing and Garby was slewed sideways to the left. Then she was banging and bumping along sideways now, right wing leading, quickly slicing through more crazy, bleating, running sheep that had no idea of which way to turn or what was happening to them. It was carnage.

3.6: Rings drilled by number 1 Prop into the Lone Oak.
(Picture; Jim Rider 2014)

Blood in the field

As Charles ran the 300 metres following the plane across the field, he saw the first blood. There were pieces of sheep everywhere. Garby had scythed through some of the flock who had gathered near an oak tree. Half a sheep's severed head had shot away fifty yards to land in mud. Another was so cleanly cut from nose to tail that Doctor Jeremy later described it as a 'perfect sagittal section' (Note 3.6) and one of which a master butcher would have been proud. Bodies of dead and dying sheep lay all around and Charles pitied them but kept pounding on towards the plane. He would now be facing human bodies, for surely no one could have survived the impact.

Edwin Locke was running down the slope as fast as he could through Coronation Meadow towards the Lone Oak, the substantial tree that Garby had just hit. The race horses were now away to his right and galloping out of harm's way. Garby was still sliding sideways towards the railway embankment and looked as if she would go straight through it. All around him on the grass were bits of his sheep, but one was still on its feet and looking at him, blinking, but with only one eye; half of its head had been cut away. Propeller blades lay among the sheep.

More sheep blood splattered against the fuselage and spilled onto the green grass as Garby headed sideways towards the edge of the field some 200 yards away. With the nose short of the eastern fence, twenty feet from the old, low, railway embankment (Fix 1.2), she finally came to rest, her final landing successfully completed. She was facing north-east on 074 degrees, and pointing towards the village of Wiggaton. (Fix 3.10.)

She comes to rest

In the plane suddenly it was all over; they had come to rest. There were a few seconds of silence. They were alive. Having held herself together and despite all the odds, Garby seemed to let out a final sigh and she gave up her magnificent struggle, her human cargo intact, babies and all.

Ahead, the old railway line, still bemoaning the loss of its trains, seemed not in the slightest bit concerned by the dramatic and fussy arrival of this ridiculous contraption that did not even have wheels. Tomorrow a woman would visit the site to see what had happened and she would become the only major casualty of the whole sorry drama – she would slide down the railway embankment and break a rib.

As he panted up to the aircraft now at the fence, Charles was expecting the worst. The time was now 2056 and Garby had been on the ground for three minutes. The forward door on the port side began to move, but only a little, as if it was jammed and unable to freely open. The air pressure was equalizing. From inside the plane he heard nothing but silence and there was silence all around except for the plaintive calling of the surviving sheep.

In the distance over towards the farm the race horses were skittish and running around in circles. The smell of hot engines was in the air. Now some voices came from inside the plane. A man said emotionally, several times, '… not filled me up properly…'

There was life after all. The door was rattled from inside and now slowly began to open. Standing in the doorway was a grey-haired man, his eyes wide, hands shaking and his face the colour of death. It was Geoffrey Whittaker and he was sweating profusely. Charles faced him.

'Who's flying this thing?' Charles demanded crossly.

He felt anger and was outraged at what he saw as

unbelievable incompetence. 'This is not Exeter airport you know! You just killed all these sheep.'

His emotions, together with the heat in his body and muscles, worked together to produce anger that he rarely felt.

'Who are you?' Charles fought to control himself.

Geoffrey stared, 'I'm Captain Whittaker.'

The truth, not apparent to Charles, was in fact that what had just taken place in the air over the Alder Grove and in Coronation Meadow was undoubtedly one of the finest examples of masterful aviation that had ever taken place. Geoffrey Whittaker had entered the ranks of superb aviators and deserved the wide acclaim that he was later to receive. What he was receiving now was the admonition of a panting, cross young man.

Whittaker was badly shocked and he was still shaking – his shirt sweat-stained, his eyes wide and staring. Inside the aircraft before opening the door he and the co-pilot had walked the length of the cabin and found none of the passengers injured. As he passed along the aisle the captain repeatedly said, 'Those Spanish bastards did not fill me up properly!'

He was convinced that he knew the cause of the crash. Now, five minutes after the plane had come to a stop, he was at the forward door of the plane looking down at a cross young man and almost in a trance-like state. He was deeply shocked, surprised to be alive but still functioning. He was still – the pilot.

'It's alright, it's alright. We are all down in one piece,' Whittaker said, mainly to himself.

He was not capable at that moment of being annoyed with Charles, nor anyone except the Spanish bowser crew.

Charles, now calmer, looked up at him and asked, 'What shall I do? Is anyone hurt? My dad's a doctor and he is coming down.'

Around the plane, now mingling with the lingering hot smell of the engines, was another unmistakable and nauseous smell – the stinking odour of overflowing drains. The holding tank from the toilets had been ruptured by the impact and the contents were on the move inside the cabin. The passengers, now calling to each other elated and disbelieving at their good fortune, pressed to the fore and aft doors keen to exchange the now offensive cabin air for the sweet Devon variety in the field outside.

When Edwin Locke arrived, gasping for breath, stewardesses were helping as, one by one, all the passengers clambered down the four foot drop from the door sills to the field. Some just sat on the grass looking at the broken plane. Some became animated and silly. Others moved a hundred metres away, convinced the danger was not yet over and stood looking back at the plane. A woman lit a cigarette with shaking fingers, but no one thought to warn her of the possible danger of igniting fuel vapour that might have been in the air. The Spanish domestics clamoured around their new hero Geoffrey and kissed him excitedly. Geoffrey hardly noticed them or their hugs and wet lips.

Still dazed Geoffrey walked around the plane checking for fire and leaks. He found none so went back inside where he sat alone in the cockpit, staring at the gauges and collecting his thoughts. He shed tears and although he was a hardened professional, he felt uncontrollably emotional. Somehow he had saved his own and sixty-one other lives but he was not quite sure how. Inside he was in turmoil and needed time to collect his thoughts and regain control of his emotions. The fire brigade found him still there half an hour later. Bill had given him a cigarette. The passengers and crew were safe. The forced landing had been a complete success. Geoffrey was, for the moment, a hero.

Several children were crying and badly shaken. One was sick over her brother but others thought it all a grand adventure, laid on for their amusement. A mother sat on the grass, clutched her baby closely to her and cried gently, kissing the little one over and over, tears falling from her cheeks onto the baby's forehead.

Two inquisitive boys ran around checking all the hot engines until their father told them to 'come away'. The time was twelve minutes past nine. An ambulance had arrived and the fire brigades were on their way. The Fluxton Lane was becoming blocked with cars, their occupants from Ottery and Tipton coming to help or view the strange events oddly unfolding near their communities. People were now coming quickly across the fields towards the scene from cottages along the lane.

Charles set to work inside Garby with the stewardesses, Sue and Sandra. Passengers wanted their bags and belongings brought out – an angry lady demanded that her umbrella be fetched together with her 200 duty free cigarettes. Charles did as he was told and brought them out to her and did not think it unusual, as if people always retrieved cigarettes and umbrellas after air crashes. Sue and Sandra were themselves quite shocked and not the cheerful girls they had been in the air. They worked quietly and slowly, stopping every now and again, when nobody was looking, to give each other a reassuring smile and once a hug.

At 2107 Ann Bradshaw-Smith arrived, followed a few minutes later by Doctor Jeremy clutching his medical bag. Robert was already there and was helping Charles. Jeremy set to work checking everyone and looking for those most in need of his help. As he moved around it quickly became obvious that there were no serious injuries – a few minor bruises only. His only immediate medical concern was for the unborn baby of a heavily pregnant woman – he felt that the bumping and seat belt pressures might have hurt the baby or brought on premature labour but the mother seemed to be unhurt. Jeremy decided that he needed to examine her quickly.

The fire brigade arrived at around 2115, rushed at the plane, ran out their hoses and looked for the fire, which they assumed to be inevitable, shouting instructions to everyone. Charles was given a brief and firm lecture and told to clear off. He thought of his dad's advice, which he had heard many times – 'Son, never expect fair play. You will be disappointed.'

Charles was not upset by this treatment at all – he did not expect any praise or thanks but neither did he expect to be given a flea in his ear by an excited fireman.

Picking up the last of the bags, Charles gently laid it on the grass beside the mother cuddling her baby. He touched her lightly and reassuringly on the shoulder for a second and then walked away home. His cold dinner would have been waiting for him if it had not been eaten by the dog.

3.7: No place for a lamb when Garby arrived.
She would not have survived here. The Lone Oak is just behind her.
(Jim Rider photo, 2014)

3.8: One of the first pictures taken after the landing.
Approx. 2200, 17th July 1980.
(Chris Saunders Collection)

3.9: G-ARBY faces 074 degrees (towards the village of Wiggaton). Mid-morning on Friday 18th July, 1980.
(Picture; Peter Harris collection).

3.10: G-ARBY Engines 4 and 3. Friday 18th July 1980.
(Annie Trimmer collection)

3.11: The 1980 Ottery St Mary Fire Engine.
But when did it arrive at the incident?
(Picture; Chris Saunders)

4

Going nowhere

On East Hill / Spread the word / Emma helps and Les looks on / The Brigade arrives… but when? / Anxious to help / Meet Annie Trimmer /The scene from 'White Cross' /To the hotel / Questions and frustrations / Party time for some, but not for the Doctor

On East Hill

If you knew well the area to the east of the River Otter and south of Ottery St Mary and had been able to see into the future, and by seeing known that the events previously described were about to happen, you might well have made your way to the southerly end of the high ridge known as East Hill. Here you would find a charming view-point called 'White Cross', which provides a magnificent panorama to the west and presents, for the visitor's enjoyment, some of Devon's finest countryside (Pic 4.1). Before you lies a winding river, rolling fields, hedgerows, lanes and in the distance the rising tors of Dartmoor. It is a quiet spot, unless perhaps a gale has blown in from the west to disturb the tranquillity. It is a popular place for walkers to perhaps pause a moment to catch their breath and marvel at all that is laid out before them. Others will picnic on the verge – others will be on the verge – dogs will be feverish at the prospect of 'walkies' and leap from the backs of cars. Perhaps in the evening young lovers might meet to enjoy private moments of romance. How lovely it is there on East Hill.

This evening you would have seen, to your right and beyond the river, the silent Garby float in over the woods in the distance. But then again, simply by the mischance of glancing briefly in another direction you would have missed it. Then your attention would certainly have been drawn by a loud and resounding 'thump' and you would have seen the dust cloud rise as the star of this show, our Garby, ended her flying career in a most spectacular manner. It wasn't her fault, poor old girl, but 'that's life', as Esther used to tell us.

Shadows would have been falling by now and in the sky heavy, grey cloud stopped the last rays of the setting sun from breaking through to illuminate the scene. Dusk – the gloaming, dimpsey, twilight – with night time just over the horizon and around the corner. Thirty years earlier in Ottery the lamplighter would have been doing his rounds and the children dawdling home to bed.

We do not know if anyone did see the events unfold before them from this good vantage point but we suspect not. At least there are no reports of such observations in the public domain so far. However one of the several witnesses on record to having seen Garby fly along the course of Longdogs Lane was already bustling his family into his car

4.1: View from White Cross on East Hill, showing key sites of the
G-ARBY landing, 17th July 1980.
(Jim Rider photo, 2014)

in Slade Close and would soon be driving up the hill. The
Nicholl family was on the way and we will soon join them
back at the White Cross view point.

Spread the word

The news of the 'crash', for that is what everyone expected,
was quickly abroad in Ottery. Phones were ringing, doors
were being knocked and neighbours were telling neighbours.

'There's a plane down near the bridge!'

Within a few repetitions this had become 'a big plane
has crashed on the cricket pitch and they are all dead.'

A local reporter was already on the case. Good citizens left their houses and made their way down towards the river wondering if they could help. Curious folk ran to see what had happened and some had heard the distant bang of the impact. Soon someone – who had been phoned by a friend at Tipton, to the south – told a neighbour that 'a big plane was down in Carter's field and the sheep are all dead!'

At the flight control centre at Exeter Airport frustrated staff were trying to work out where the plane might be down. No member of the public had yet rung in to give this vital information. Retained and Reserve Fire Crews were rapidly mustering at their stations but they needed to be given the exact location of the aircraft. The only known fact at this stage was from Whittaker's Mayday and that said that Garby was turning south over Ottery. But how far on had she glided? The decision was taken to send the crews to Tipton. Eventually, about twenty minutes after the landing, blue lights were flashing in the streets of Ottery and heading down the lane towards the Salston Hotel and Tipton St John. A fire engine and ambulance were coming from Sidmouth and several more appliances and ambulances were on their way from Exeter.

Emma helps and Les looks on

Emma Bradshaw-Smith was playing her part in the rescue operation and was standing anxiously at the farm gate as requested to do so by her father (Fix 3.6). She had opened the gate and was anxiously waiting for an emergency vehicle of some sort to arrive. The time was now between five and ten past nine and Garby had been on the ground for around fifteen minutes. Further back up the lane a few cars had arrived at another open field gate (Fix 4.1) and had driven into the field. The occupants were standing outside their vehicles looking downhill towards the plane just under half a mile away.

One of these drivers was Les Carter, a local newsagent and, incidentally, no relation to Oliver Carter. He lived in Ottery and was driving home from Exeter. As he drove down Barrack Road, heading downhill towards the river, he saw what he mistook for a bus taking an unusual route. He quickly realised that it was a plane passing low near the cricket field as it turned left towards the hotel. He followed it and turned right into Strawberry Lane, passed the Salston Hotel on his left and, after driving about 300 yards, pulled into a field from where he had a view of Garby that, by the time he arrived, was at the far edge of Coronation Meadow almost half a mile away. Les stood and watched the scene for at least ten minutes and when he was sure that all the people were off the plane he returned to his car and drove home up the lane he had come down, again passing the hotel.

The reason I am relating Les' view of events is because it adds a bit of fuel – oh for some more fuel where it was needed in this tale – to an interesting difference of accounts. Les is able to account for at least twenty minutes of eye contact time with the plane. He is adamant that at no time did he see, hear, or pass a fire engine on either of his drives up or down the lane. We know that he saw the plane in the air at 2052 and twenty minutes after that is, of course 2112, and by that time Emma had probably already been waiting at the other gate further down the lane for about five minutes. Both Emma and Les report that no fire engines were in the field at that time (2112). Dr Jeremy also states very positively that the fire engine was not at Garby as he arrived and he could not have been there before 2112 (see Chapter 3).

The Brigade arrives… but when?

To be fair to the Ottery St Mary Fire Brigade they are not on public record as claiming that they arrived at Garby at any particular time. Which leaves us wondering why several press reports published in the following few days report that the Ottery Brigade was '… at the scene within three minutes of touchdown'. Well they certainly were not. To have achieved that remarkable feat they would have needed at least twenty minutes advance warning and to have been parked up, all booted and helmeted, at the Salston Hotel ready for action.

The Ottery brigade was a 'retained' group of trained volunteers and the men took a commendable pride in doing their dangerous and challenging job well. Everyone is and was proud of them. We all know that fire brigade crews take pride in turning out very quickly and that a rapid response time is vitally important as it can mean the difference between life and death for someone trapped in a fire.

The previous evening had seen a practise drill at the small fire station in Batt's Lane (Fix 4.2)(Pic 4.2). By the way, this must be one of the worst locations for a fire station in Devon and possibly the world – unless there was perhaps a fire in the adjacent United Reformed Church or the London Inn just up the road! You could hardly fit your bike down the lanes and a baby in a pram would have no trouble in clobbering both walls on opposite sides of the road with his rattles simultaneously. (Well alright then, that is a bit of a fun exaggeration but it is not more than eight feet wide and I couldn't drive down it all the other evening due to a car parked half on the pavement and scaffolding against one of the houses.)

At 2051, as Garby was gliding overhead, Sub Officer Edgar Hawkins, ignorant of this singular aviation event, was at his desk in the station writing up his report on the previous evening's training. Some minutes later – we don't know exactly when – Frank Bastin, one of his trusty firemen, burst into the office panting:

'… Plane crashing, let's go!'

'Where to?' asks Edgar.

'Salston by the look of it.'

Frank had been near his house in Little Close just off Winter's Lane talking to a neighbour when they both saw the Viscount flying over the town. Frank immediately ran the few yards to his house and jumped on his motorbike. He set off for the fire station, around a quarter of a mile away. As he clattered away (at probably around 2058) his neighbour called to Frank telling him that 'the plane turned left towards the Salston and soon after that there had been a big thump and then a bang.'

At around 2100, according to Edgar Hawkins' account,

no alert had yet come through from Exeter Fire HQ but the flight controller had by this time been aware of the key Mayday facts for at least ten minutes. That previous sentence is one of the most significant in this book in understanding just what actually did happen on that summer's evening. Did something go wrong? Was there a system failure of some sort?

One by one more of the crew ran in from their homes or wherever they were across the town. Edgar was now convinced that there was an incident in progress and he initiated the call out pager response system alerting all his firemen. He also sounded an alarm at Fire HQ. So all of the crew members who had gone to the fire station must have either seen Garby overhead or were immediately told of the imminent crash by someone who had seen the plane gliding in the air. All the firemen who responded and rushed to the fire station did so *before* they were bleeped on their pagers.

4.2: The old fire station in Batts Lane.
(Jim Rider photo, 2014)

To move off to the incident, Edgar needed a crew of six including himself. The five whom he now had opened the doors, ran up the motor on the appliance and threw on their suits, helmets and boots. Frank Bastin cannot say at what time he arrived at the fire station but he is adamant that he was on the fire engine and away within about three minutes of his arrival. It is also important to remember that at this point Edgar could only guess at where he thought the plane might be on the ground. He did not know where it was; he had not yet been given a 'fix'.

The gate to Coronation Meadow was a whole 1.59 miles away and traffic was light. According to Les Carter the lanes were not yet blocked with traffic or sightseers – that would happen later. I safely did a test drive of the route and, keeping within the speed limits, it took me a little more than four minutes to drive from the old fire station to the gate into the field. I did this test at the same time in the evening that the fire engine did the drive; traffic was light and I was not held up. It would be reasonable to assume that the fire engine would have been able to reduce my time by possibly thirty seconds, but there are several tight bends to negotiate so it may have taken them longer than my four minutes.

So if it wasn't 'three minutes', how quickly did the Ottery Fire Brigade get to Garby? Well I calculate that they arrived after 2114, probably 2115 (as stated in Chapter 3), but possibly as late as 2120. So it's closer to half an hour rather than ten minutes after Garby landed. We don't know and never will. We need to remember that the Mayday went out from Garby at 2050. But Edgar Hawkins did tell our researcher that his fellow firemen had witnessed the aircraft, which immediately caused them to rush from their homes around the town and converge on the station, and it was only a minute or so before the first five of the station complement of twelve personnel had arrived and, grabbing their uniforms and helmets, clambered aboard the fire engine alongside their Chief.

Once the fire appliance was on the road, Edgar radioed the Devon Fire Service Head Quarters at Clyst St George to report that they were on the way to the incident. He was told that reports had just started coming in and that the Ottery crew were to make for Strawberry Lane with all speed. The crew had seen enough to have a pretty good idea of where the airliner might have come down and consequently they spotted it after driving past the Salston Manor Hotel. They entered the field through a farm gate held open by an anxious young lady (this was Emma Bradshaw-Smith). They raced across the field to where the aircraft had finally come to rest and, as they did so, they ignored the frantic waves of Sunshine Locke.

Anxious to help

Back in Ottery, the nurses based at the town's Cottage Hospital were ringing each other because one of them had been alerted to the plane crash. Soon several nurses were moving to the small local hospital where the senior nurse telephoned the Exeter Emergency Centre to report that they were standing by to receive casualties if required.

As all farmers know their land, so Sunshine knew this field; like the back of his hand. He knew every dip, every fence post, every tree. He also knew the soft bits where water would collect, for Coronation Meadow was never either completely boggy or completely dry. When Garby hit the ground she hit dry ground hard, hence the 'bang' described by Doctor Jeremy and soon there was a 'dust cloud rising' he reports. However within a few metres and around the Lone Oak, there were boggy conditions and mud.

There were also traps for tractors, and indeed fire engines, in Coronation Meadow in the form of manholes and beneath them lay a drainage system to keep the field from becoming very boggy after rain (Pic 4.3). Sunshine tried to warn the fire engine driver of the manholes but the latter was determined to get to Garby as quickly as he could so Sunshine was ignored and the driver headed straight for the plane. Fortunately the appliance narrowly missed several of the covers and did not get bogged down in the wet places. By the way, Sunshine has claimed all through my investigations that the first on scene after the landing was John Boyce closely followed by Sunshine himself. John Boyce says that the first door of the plane he saw open was the rear door and a chute was being used on which passengers were sliding the four foot drop down to the ground.

Another witness to the actual landing was Jeff Rowland, a forty-three-year-old local farm worker. Jeff had been working outside his cottage in nearby Salston Barton when he saw Garby just clear the Salston Manor Hotel and come in low over the fields. On the day after the event he told a local reporter, 'One engine had

4.3: Coronation Meadow manhole.
(Jim Rider photo, 2014)

stopped, and it turned as it went overhead, and then flew on over the Salston Hotel, barely missing it. Then it went out of sight and there was a crash like a tree falling as it went down. I ran down to the field where it had crashed and the passengers had got out and walked away. It was incredible. One wing had been ripped off and four sheep in the field had been killed, but no one was killed or badly injured. Everyone was badly shocked and dazed but it was a marvellous bit of flying to get it down in one piece like that.' *(Quotes used with kind permission and by courtesy of the Express and Echo, Exeter.)*

A passenger on the plane, Mr Harold Matthews, a thirty-eight-year-old company director from Cheltenham claimed that some of the passengers were screaming as the plane came down. He was reported as saying 'After the crash it was difficult to make them calm down enough to let us all get out. The panic was so bad at one stage that they would have trampled kids to get to the doors. That's finished me. I will never fly again. It was the first flight for my children, and I won't let them fly again until they are old enough to make up their own minds. We just had time to brace ourselves before hitting the field. The plane bounced three of four times and everything started to come apart. Two or three windows burst and everything fell out of the cupboards.'

Eye witness to the crash Mrs Lilly Lock (Note 4.1) of Burnt House Cottage, Fluxton, was at home and saw most of the landing. Her cottage overlooks the meadow. She told the Pulmans News reporter:

'I was so frightened by the crash that I thought something was landing from outer space. I was burning rubbish out the back when I suddenly heard this funny noise like whistling… racehorses went one way, bullocks the other; sheep went berserk. I saw the plane come down among them. It appeared to tip over but this was as it was slewing around. I heard shouts and screams for help. My son Edwin went to the nearby farm for help and they quickly went down to the place. Within minutes there were fire engines and ambulances everywhere. I've never seen anything like it.' *(Quote used with kind permission and by courtesy of Pulmans News.)*

Meet Annie Trimmer

The farm house at Bishop's Court Farm (Fix 4.3) is the closest residence to the place where Garby had come to rest.

The pleasant, traditional style house faces north and from the upper rooms a glimpse of Garby could be had through the line of trees, down the slope towards the winding River Otter. Here lived John Carter (Note 4.2) with his three children, Andrew, Paul and the youngest, Ann, aged nine.

Also living in the farmhouse with the family was Annie Trimmer, John's housekeeper. Annie was and still is an active, able and busy person and was soon to play a big part in events. John's father, Oliver Carter, managed the farm firmly and efficiently although he did not live in the farmhouse. Oliver was well known locally as a good farmer. He was not someone who was ever in much doubt about where his next course of action lay. Whilst he could best be described by those who knew him well as a 'bit tetchy' he could also turn on the charm when he needed to do so. He loved his three grandchildren and they loved to spend time with him.

Coronation Meadow had originally been a southerly continuation of the Alder Grove but most of its trees had been cleared to provide pasture and grazing with only the oak trees left untouched. The clearance work had taken several years of hard graft. Trees were cleared and a complex drainage system had been laid to improve the ground quality. Trenches were dug, pipes installed, manholes bricked into the soft ground. This work had mostly been done by John and Oliver Carter and their stalwart and loyal farmhand, Sunshine Locke.

The Lone Oak, which features strongly in this tale, might well have been cleared with many other trees but it had been left untouched until it was eventually marked so uniquely by Garby.

Oliver had Sunshine also clear the meadow of stones and this he did most carefully, taking more than six months to complete the task. When the ground was eventually cleared, Oliver used the land as a gallop and exercise area for his race horses, and he also let the local riders use the area freely for their Point to Point events. Oliver's most famously successful race horse, 'Ottaway', was stabled at the farm.

At the time of the landing, Annie was at home putting young Ann to bed when the phone rang. A neighbour said excitedly, 'Annie… there is a bloody great plane down in your field!'

The time was now a few minutes before nine o'clock and Annie had been planning to get Ann to bed before then so that she could watch 'Edward and Mrs Simpson' on TV. Ann however, as is usual with little girls at bed time, had not been in a particular hurry. Annie quickly put the phone down and rushed outside to see if she could see the plane and was horrified to see it down at the bottom of the meadow. Five valuable racehorses were galloping around snorting and at risk of injuring themselves.

Annie called up the stairs telling young Ann to get dressed. One of the boys had been out playing cricket; the other helping his dad up in the fields.

Annie was anxious.

'Ann – get dressed quickly, there's an emergency in the meadow. I need you to help me round up the horses.'

They both pulled on some boots and made their way down into the field and started trying to catch and calm the five horses. Sheep were standing around at the top of the field bleating and Ann could see some sheep lying still on the grass in the distance.

Annie remembers hearing sirens in the lane. Ambulances were coming from all directions and the first one soon arrived but as yet there was no sign of a fire engine. Annie thinks that the time then was around ten past nine. Like Sunshine Locke, Annie was also concerned about the ambulances coming to grief in the manholes and did her best to wave the drivers away and warn them. The manholes were not easy to see in the grass. A police car soon arrived and at the plane Annie thought she could see the pilots helping the passengers out onto the grass.

The scene from White Cross

In Slade Close, Alan Nicholl was bundling his children, Karen aged fourteen and Timothy, nine, into the family car. They set off up to East Hill Strips and to a vantage point at the southern end of the ridge where the lane bears to the left towards Sidbury about two miles away. This is the very spot that I described in the opening paragraph of this chapter and is known as White Cross (Fix 4.4). Alan was hoping that he and the family would have a good view of the action taking place across the River Otter where he had calculated that the plane must have come down.

They were not disappointed for in the distance and deepening gloom there were lots of emergency vehicles gathering, their blue lights flashing and sirens wailing. It was quite a spectacle. But the family did not stay long as Timothy was in his pyjamas and after a long day at school thought he would rather be in bed. So after a few minutes they went home and on the way Alan had another idea on how he might keep in touch with events – his short wave radio.

To the hotel

By half past nine at least eight fire appliances of the Devon Fire Service were in the field. Chief Superintendent Colin Evans, head of Exeter Police, arrived to take charge of operations. Soon dozens of police from Ottery, Honiton, Sidmouth, Exmouth and Exeter were on the scene as well as more than fifty firemen with eight fire engines and six ambulances. Police officers were sent to keep the lanes clear for the emergency services. Staff from the Salston Manor Hotel arrived in their own vehicle and the proprietor, Neils Svendsen, offered any assistance that the police might require and it was immediately decided that the hotel would be the operations base and incident room for the crash. The hotel manageress, Nicola Hill, aged twenty-two, stayed in the field helping and comforting passengers and then she went back to the hotel to make preparations. Ambulances began ferrying passengers to the hotel and offers of help with transportation from members of the public with vehicles nearby were gratefully accepted. One of those helping was a Mr Boyes who helped with the ferrying for more than an hour.

The girl from the office, her new shoes now scratched, dusty and forgotten but still on her feet, had banged her arm in the crash. Her young man helped her into an ambulance even though she protested and said he was fussing her. He set off across the field on foot but was stopped by a kindly policeman who helped him into a Land Rover with some of the Spanish domestics. Off they all went happily enough to the Salston Hotel three quarters of a mile away, avoiding Sunshine's manholes.

Back home in Slade Close, Alan Nicholl tuned in his short wave radio and heard someone, probably the police, say '… and customs are on their way.' He thought, *Well they never miss a trick.*

Indeed they did not and officers were checking the plane on the evening of the crash. (Pic 5.2.)

Some reports say that eleven passengers were taken to the Royal Devon and Exeter hospital and of those two were detained overnight, but Dr Jeremy Bradshaw-Smith is quite certain that that did not happen. One newspaper reported that a woman was taken to hospital with a neck injury. This was Mrs Patricia Meller and her daughter, Siobhan, also confirms that she, then aged nine, and her step-father were guests at the hotel for four nights. During that time they were provided with taxis to the hospital so that they could visit the casualty. However Dr Jeremy was mainly concerned about the pregnant passenger, Mrs Muriel Quartermain of Oxford, and asked Mr Boyes to take her to his house so that he could assess if she was injured.

Jeremy went with her but you can read an interesting and surprising twist involving this lady later in this chapter… no, she didn't have the baby in a Land Rover!

Several accounts of an odd event, which probably happened at the plane sometime after half past nine, or even nearer ten o'clock, when it had become quite dark apart from the flood lights, concerned the baggage. Most of the bags had already been taken up to the hotel but it was reported that a man was seen scampering away from the plane in the dark illuminated momentarily by the flood lights. He was carrying two suitcases. He had entered the hold of the plane and a few minutes later emerged carrying these personal belongings. It is most unlikely that this was a returned passenger as they were all by this time in the hotel and unlikely to have had the motivation to return. The plane itself was being watched by the fire crew and the police were in attendance.

The team of customs officers that had been sent to the incident from Exeter would have had the usual interest in incoming bags, and also the 'bar boxes', which the plane carried. However these customs officers were in uniform and they would have had no reason to go scampering away with a case or two. Could this have been one of the many gawpers who were now peering over the hedge on the Tipton lane and over the fence by the railway embankment? I like to think, just for fun, that this might have been a man from Beer or Budleigh who was possibly the great, great grandson of a smuggler or even a passing Cornish wrecker. If he was he could never have come from squeaky-clean Sidmouth I fancy. Sub Fire Officer Edgar Hawkins gave chase, retrieved the bags and replaced them in the aircraft.

Furthermore, on the dark side of things back in the field, a vet had been called to despatch some still suffering sheep.

John Carter was arranging for the carcasses to be put to the useful purpose of providing food for local dogs, possibly the hounds belonging to the local hunt. It would have been very surprising if a couple of chops, a spare rib or a leg of lamb had not found their way to a table or two for Sunday lunch over the coming weekend.

Earlier at the hotel there had inevitably been considerable alarm when the gliding aircraft had passed overhead at around sixty feet above the high chimney pots. These tall, thin structures, together with the rich red brickwork gave the hotel character and grandeur in the manner of an imposing country seat. The chimneys seemed to be challenging any approaching thunder storm to do its worst but as far as is known none has ever done so.

In the hotel pool and on the patio, guests had looked up curiously at Garby's underbelly and quickly realised that some sort of disaster was imminent. Immediately shouts of alarm were heard and those who had not seen the plane ran outside to see what they could. A guest who was in the squash court, Stuart McCulloch, ran out shouting, 'A plane is crashing!'

Nicola Hill, the duty manager, had been talking to guests in the bar and she immediately said, 'I must go, please excuse me.'

She collected the hotel's first aid box and ran outside where she was joined by other members of the staff, manager Peter Feather and chef Andrew Roberts. Then she drove them in the hotel Land Rover down to the field. At the plane she offered passengers lifts up to the hotel and assisted the ambulance crews with the evacuation.

As the passengers arrived at the hotel they were still dazed and coming to terms with their horrific experience in Coronation Meadow less than thirty minutes previously. They were beginning to realise how lucky they were to be alive; they were badly shocked and shaking, their pulses still racing. Kindly hotel guests gathered round and took them to comfortable chairs and sofas where bustling waitresses brought tea, coffee and biscuits.

The ballroom was quickly turned into a first aid centre manned by ambulance crews. A few passengers had cuts and bruises but there was very little first aid to be done.

The hotel – a comfortable three star establishment with a good reputation – had around thirty bedrooms. Many guests came regularly to enjoy the surrounding countryside, beaches and east Devon attractions.

The police set up their incident room in the library and telephones were brought in. The police inspector, well trained professional that he was, and the senior fire officer, were realising that this incident could have been much worse and that not only had the passengers but also the people in the hotel, and indeed much of the population of Ottery, got away with things lightly. The pilot had surely done a magnificent job but why was there no fire? Where was all the fuel? Soon a phone call from London advised Chief Superintendent Colin Evans that the Air Accident Investigators were on their way. Perhaps that would have been a good moment to talk to Oliver Carter of Bishop's Court Farm but he did not do so and already Oliver was grumpy, to put it mildly.

In the bar and lounge the passengers began talking

urgently, 'I knew we were crashing… it was awful but no one panicked you know.'

'No, no one did.'

'We are so lucky; we are here, and alive.'

And so it went on as more and more passengers arrived in the six ambulances, which then returned to the field to continue their ferry duties. More tea was brought and the level of the conversation rose, the passengers taking comfort from the nearness of others and the noise and clamour. In the kitchen, Andrew Roberts was seeing what was to be done and chambermaids were being called in from the town to help upstairs with setting up bedrooms.

The children were now there as well and, as children will always do, they found something with which to play and made a game of hide and seek behind the sofas. Neils Svendsen, the owner, and the staff were all kindness, compassion and generosity. Nothing was too much trouble and all the hot drinks, biscuits and soon some cake as well, were free. Then someone, it might have been one of the retained fire crews, said, 'Actually if there was something stronger that would be good.'

Out came the stronger drinks and before anyone could say, 'mine's a chimney pot!!' a bit of a knees-up party was in the making.

Outside in the lane, traffic and sightseers were now blocking the way down to the crash. The police were trying to move everyone along but it was becoming difficult to make a way through for the ambulances and for the stood-down fire appliances that were trying to return to their bases. 'There's a cuppa in the hotel before you go,' called a Policeman to a fire engine driver.

So the big red machine with its crew turned in and parked in front of the hotel with the others. What a sight it all was.

'A party? Where?'

'They are all in the bar.'

Down in the field, Edgar Hawkins had decided that he and his crew would keep watch over his charge by night and had arranged for a few more crew members to come over from Ottery to relieve the original crew, so that they could go home for a meal break. This they did and returned in about an hour. The Ottery crew kept guard with the fire engine in attendance all through the night even though there was virtually no chance of a fire.

Questions and frustrations

Say what you will about the press in general and reporters in particular but you have to hand it to them for speed, determination and tenacity when they smell a good story. A plane crash, no matter what the outcome, is always a good story. This one was 'hot' and it 'had legs' – press jargon for – it was going to be a good story for ongoing news value, discussion and 'fall out'. Someone must have messed up. Someone had indeed, but whom?

Despite spending several hours on the question of how the press got hold of Shirley Whittaker's phone number within an hour of the crash, I cannot arrive at an answer, but they did just that. The first Shirley heard of the serious incident involving her husband was when her telephone rang at around ten o'clock on the evening of the crash and one of the press pack began asking her questions about Geoff. The press were mainly after the human angle: where did he live? When did she see him last? Where had they taken him? When was she expecting him home? The questions came tumbling at her. All she wanted to do was to talk to someone at Alidair and find out if Geoff was injured but as soon as she put the phone down at the end of a call it rang again with another reporter asking the same questions.

She was distraught and this went on for an hour or so before Geoff eventually managed to get through and talk to her from the Exeter control room where he was now being held by the police for questioning. He told her that he was unhurt but shaken and that he had already demanded that the bowser at Santander be dipped and the quantity of litres it held recorded.

'It wasn't my fault,' he told her.

At last she knew that he was alright but that was not until around midnight. She stayed up all night as sleep was impossible. Even the dogs in the house sensed that something was wrong.

Party time for some, but not for the Doctor

With the drinks flowing and more food appearing there was soon a full scale party underway in the public areas of the hotel. Even those who were not taking alcohol, particularly those members of the emergency services who had not yet been stood down, were soaking up the 'happy to be alive' atmosphere. The group had overflowed into the lounge and everyone was swapping experiences, asking questions and talking loudly. Someone put some dancing music on the hi-fi. There was a lot of laughter and the press were doing their best to corner passengers who were happy to relate their experiences to a wider audience. These were the days before the concept of paparazzi swarming over an event with their cameras of course, so not surprisingly I have only been able to trace one picture taken at the hotel that evening. It shows Betty Svendsen talking to two passengers (Pic. 4.4).

SPANISH passengers on the crashed aircraft, Mrs. Maria Pilar Quindimil with her husband, Manuel, talk to a director of the Salston Hotel, Mrs. Elizabeth Svendsen, left, about their escape. Also in the picture, second left, is Maria Vasquez, a Spanish waitress at the hotel.

4.4: Mrs E Svendsen (left) talks to passengers shortly after the landing.
(Used by kind permission of 'Express and Echo')

Doctor Jeremy and his wife, Ann, had checked Muriel Quartermain at his house just a hundred yards from the hotel. He was quite happy that she was not injured in any obvious way and appeared to be suffering no ill effects from the crash, other than those associated with the shock she had experienced. However he could not check the unborn baby's condition because to do so he would have needed a foetal heart monitor. His concern now was to quickly send Muriel to the main hospital at Heavitree in Exeter, and so he rang the Accident and Emergency Department there to arrange for her to be seen as soon as possible. The A and E staff were aware of the plane crash and were expecting casualties to arrive, although it was beginning to appear to them that they would not be dealing with a major incident.

The obvious thing now for Dr Jeremy to do was to run round to the hotel and arrange for one of the ambulances to take mother and unborn baby to the hospital and that is what he did. Then he had a surprise. None of the ambulance crews wanted to tear themselves away from the party! The Spanish ladies were being outrageously entertaining and really letting their hair down! He tried all of the crews and none of them would budge.

Jeremy was amazed at this behaviour that he regarded as a complete lack of professionalism. Now he found himself becoming cross; he had himself been through quite an emotional roller coaster ride in the last hour… 'Well you WILL take this patient NOW! I insist. If you don't I will personally make sure you are disciplined.' Grudgingly one of the crews acceded and moved reluctantly outside to find that their ambulance was now blocked in.

As Mrs Quartermain eventually climbed into the back of the ambulance on her way to hospital, she turned back to Jeremy and Ann and called, 'If it's a boy I'm going to call him Geoffrey after that wonderful pilot.'

How thrilling it would be all these years after the event to find out what happened to Muriel Quartermain and whether or not she was eventually safely delivered of a boy or a girl.

Then the phone rang in the Bradshaw-Smith's house. Jeremy was joint owner of a yacht that, during the evening, was being sailed from Plymouth to Dartmouth. The wind had got up and a strong, blustery south, westerly had sent lots of small boats scuttling into the south Devon harbours for shelter. Jeremy replied to the caller: 'I'm sure you will manage… I have other things on my mind just at the moment.'

About an hour later, a nurse at Heavitree rang Jeremy to let him know that mother and the unborn baby were fine despite some mild bruising to Muriel. At last Jeremy could relax but the family had plenty to talk and think about. It had been an unusual sort of a day.

Down in the meadow things were already not quite as they should have been. There were the bodies of four dead sheep but there were five heads. By the look of things someone had crept in under cover of darkness and helped themselves to a Sunday lunch.

4.5: Members of the Ottery St Mary fire crew who attended the incident.
Back row, from the left; Gordon Bridle, Sub Officer Edgar Hawkins,
Frank Bastin, Trevor Sprague. Front row; Percy Bridle, Chris Snow.

5

Going away

And so to bed / Friday 18th July / Sightseers arrive and Annie rakes it in / Oliver locks the gate / Garby comes apart / Annie is on parade / Garby passes away

And so to bed

In the Salston Hotel at around ten o'clock a smart coach arrived from Plymouth. It had been laid on by Brittany Ferries to take any passengers who wished to do so to travel to Plymouth where they would be accommodated. Thirty-nine passengers picked up their bags and joined the bus. Nineteen passengers remained at the Salston. Two of the passengers who chose to remain were the daughter and husband of Mrs Meller, who was being treated in the hospital in Exeter.

At half past ten, Nicola Hill decided it was time to turn off the taps and try to settle the passengers down for the night. The chambermaids had been busy and prepared as many rooms as were available. These were provided free of charge but if passengers did want to pay then that was accepted. At the reception desk the family groups collected their keys and the parents took their children upstairs to try to settle them for sleep. Then the elderly sisters were given a twin room and so were the stewardesses, Sue and Sandra, who, everyone agreed, had done magnificently well during the whole drama.

The receptionist worked on down the list and there was just one room left as the young couple came to the desk. Emotionally, having survived the crash, they were now much closer to each other, almost as if they were married.

'Well I only have a double left I'm afraid,' said the receptionist with the keys, smiling inquisitively.

'Would you two mind sharing?'

'No, not at all, we can manage. That will be fine.'

The key was handed over, and up between the ornately carved banisters went the happy couple. They held hands and whispered to each other as they climbed the richly carpeted staircase.

Soon after 2200 the two pilots had arrived at Exeter Airport and were making their way to the office of the Managing Director of Exeter Airport Ltd, the company that ran the airport. Two miles away to the west, rooms were being prepared for them at the Gypsy Hill Hotel at Pinhoe, but there were to be a couple of hours of questioning before Geoff and Bill would be able to go there. A press photographer arrived hoping for an opportunity to get some pictures of the pilots in time for tomorrow's editions of the nationals but he was sent packing. Geoff tried to telephone

Shirley in Jersey several times but her phone was continually engaged. The press were on the case.

The Managing Director and owner of Alidair, Roger Dadd, rang and Geoff talked to him briefly giving him an outline report of what had happened. Dadd said he was glad that there were no serious injuries and that he would be in the field early the following morning. He wanted the 'Alidair Scotland' name on Garby's fuselage painted over before anyone took photos but he was already far too late with that. (Pic. 5.1.) Dadd was hoping that Alidair would come out of this mess well but he was to be disappointed.

Within the next hour the first member of the Aircraft Accident Investigation Branch (AAIB) arrived and after briefly expressing his regrets to the pilots about the unfortunate events that brought him there he proceeded to establish the facts. Pilots know full well what the AAIB procedure will be following an incident even though only a few ever experience an investigation first-hand. Every aspect will be thoroughly investigated and eventually, after a few months, a comprehensive, carefully prepared and detailed report will be produced and made available to the government, air industry and the public. It is easily found now online (Apx 1 AAIB). There was a lot of work to be done and Geoff and Bill had to co-operate fully with the investigation and they certainly did so.

Even at this early stage, Geoff was raising his suspicions about the refuelling in Santander and insisting that the Spanish bowser be checked and everything at that end of the flight thoroughly investigated, despite the international political implications. That was duly noted by the investigator.

5.1: Garby at around 2230 on 17th July 1980.

The Managing Director of the airport, Harry Ellis, a retired RAF Wing Commander and very experienced pilot, sat in on the questioning and arranged for the Approach Controller and the refuelling staff to be brought in to talk to the investigator and for fuel samples to be produced. The controller was able to describe Garby's track in from Berry Head, the Mayday and the airport's response to the forced landing. Fuel samples from the airport tank and from the bowser are always kept when an aircraft has been refuelled, and the investigator needed to take these away for analysis.

Eventually the pilots were taken to the hotel where they were able at last to talk to their families before, exhausted, they fell into bed. Tomorrow had already arrived.

We return now to Garby, lying forlornly in Oliver Carter's field. There is good evidence, in the form of a photograph, that customs officers did attend the incident soon after the landing. A picture clearly shows a customs officer at one of Garby's doors. (Pic 5.2.) They would have wanted to check all the bags of the passengers and crew and the aircraft's cabin bar boxes. After all, as far as customs Regulations went this was just another flight with duty liable goods being brought into the UK. They were responsible for checking that the duty payable was, in fact, paid.

The only difference from normal procedures for the officers concerned was that they would have to check the bags and boxes, either in the dark, in a field, or in the hotel. However, because of the distress that passengers had experienced the customs officers might well have just checked a few bags and talked sensitively to any passengers who seemed fairly in control of their emotions and, without asking, 'Do you have anything to declare?' satisfied themselves that there wasn't much duty to collect anyway and let the passengers be taken up to the hotel. None of the witnesses report seeing customs officers at the hotel. They could have popped in for drink on the house though and been a bit sociable at the party! We can't be sure about what actually happened and it remains a mystery, but eventually a passenger might be able to tell us. (Note 5.1) (Apx 1 Ottery St Mary Heritage Society).

Friday 18th July

The following morning at the Gypsy Hill Hotel, Geoff and Bill were tucking into a good old fry-up, with all the trimmings. The hotel served an excellent full English breakfast and, as they knew they were about to face another

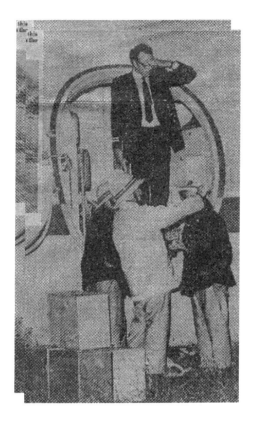

5.2: A customs officer in attendance. Probably taken late on the evening
of the landing. 17th July 1980
(Used by kind permission of 'Express and Echo')

difficult day, the pilots thought that they might just as well
get off to a good start.

After breakfast at the Salston Hotel, the nineteen
remaining passengers were hoping to have a better day than
they had experienced the day before. The *Armorique* arrived
at the Plymouth ferry terminal during the Friday afternoon
but that was not to be the end of the saga for Mr Bean who

was particularly irked at two further negative developments. Although his car and most of the family's travelling possessions were safely on the *Armorique*, the car could not be unloaded because of an electrical fault in the lift. As well as that inconvenience, Mr Bean discovered that the door key for his car had been left in Spain. He was not at all amused and caused quite a fuss in the terminal. Eventually he and the family set off for Reading.

Meanwhile in Coronation Meadow, the investigators had arrived just as dawn was breaking and were about their business. Oliver Carter was watching them suspiciously from the edge of the sixty-three acre field. He was using binoculars whilst resting his elbows on one of the farm gates. The area had been cordoned off by the police who were not letting anyone into the field except authorised officials and senior managers from Alidair Scotland, and one of their workers who was finishing painting out the airline's name with white paint.

The four man AAIB team from the Ministry of Trade had already removed the black box flight recorder from the aircraft and was conducting a close search of the field. Sheep were still around, but they mostly kept away from all the activity. As Oliver watched, a coastguard Land Rover came down the lane and an officer got out and went over to the plane. 'What had the coastguards to do with it?' wondered Oliver.

The lane was now almost jammed with cars and there were already around fifty people looking over the hedges to view the proceedings. Sunshine Locke came up to Oliver and put his hand on the gate to open it.

5.3: 'Please give generously', says Annie Trimmer (left).
(Picture 'Ottery News' 1/8/80)

'They won't want you in there, Sunshine,' grumbled Oliver.

'They do want me actually,' said Sunshine, pushing open the gate and sounding important.

'I'm to show them where I saw the plane hit the top of the tree and then crash. They want witnesses who actually saw it come down.'

Oliver stood aside and let Sunshine through.

'Tell them somebody should be asking me for their plane back. I'm over here waiting… and tell them to keep away from them manholes!'

The investigators continued their work throughout the day. The pilots arrived and climbed into Garby with one of the investigators. On the old railway embankment sightseers gathered and a press photographer was taking pictures. A lady slipped on the wet grass on the embankment, tumbled down the slope, broke a rib, and went down in the history of air crashes as the most serious injury in this particular incident. Sunshine was seen plodding around the field, pointing up at trees and walking along holding his arms out as if he was Garby herself, rocking from side to side. Two investigators with him measured everything and took notes.

Annie Trimmer arrived and said to John that she had come up with an idea. She was thinking that if any of the passengers had suffered back injuries in the crash they would need to be in hospital for some time. She thought that there might be an opportunity to collect some money from the sightseers for the Spinal Unit at Stoke Mandeville Hospital; a good cause about which she had been recently reading.

She said quietly to John, 'As there are so many sightseers why don't we sell tickets so that people can go in and see the plane properly without trying to climb over our hedges? We could get some money for Stoke Mandeville Hospital. They could drive into the field and park at the top.'

John said he would think about it and discuss it with Oliver later, but Annie thought he was immediately taken with the idea.

At around ten thirty, Oliver was nowhere to be seen but Annie felt sure that he would agree with her collection idea.

Perhaps he was down at the plane. Sightseers were still climbing on gates and hedges along the lane to try to get a decent view of the plane down at the bottom of the meadow.

Being a confident lady, Annie now took matters into her own hands and collected a couple of buckets from the shed, threw open the gates and let people into the field provided they dropped 30p into her bucket. The collection was going ahead, she just hoped Oliver would approve. For now Annie just wanted to make hay while the sun was still shining, which indeed it was, and poor old Garby was still sitting forlornly at the bottom of the meadow.

At lunch time young Ann also came up with her own idea. 'I know what I can do Annie. I'll bring up Beauty and we can give the children pony rides down to the plane. She'd love it and she won't mess up the field. Oh do say 'yes' Annie… please.'

The whole thing was becoming a grand adventure. Annie agreed and hoped Oliver was going to be in one of his charming and acquiescent moods. Fortunately he was. So Annie and Ann opened the gate. Beauty was all saddled up, the sun was out and with red and white tape surrounding Garby, the meadow had gone 'en fête' and even looked almost ready for a proper Coronation-style celebration.

In they came, a few at first and then more and more. In they came on foot from the village, from Tipton, with their cars, push chairs, bikes, grannies, dogs, mums and dads, boys and girls. One lad even brought a goldfish along in a plastic bag. 'There will be a coach trip here soon,' chuckled Annie.

The news spread quickly that the field was open to visitors and by lunch time a couple of Annie's friends arrived to help her. Photographers were literally having a 'field day'. 'Can we take pictures Miss?' enquired a young lad.

'Yes, yes of course. Help yourself. It'll be fine. Just take as many as you like.'

Momentarily she regretted her hasty response remembering that the aim was to make some money for the hospital.

Again she was forming an idea. She went and found her camera and started taking her own pictures – they would be on sale next week.

Cars were now in the field; parked on the high ground near the gate and Garby must have been feeling quite a celebrity with so much attention. People were walking around gazing, discussing, snapping away and holding little investigations of their own.

'How did it happen?'

'Wasn't anybody killed, Dad?'

'Where are the bits of the sheep Mum?'

Why do children like to be gruesome? If the railway had still been up and running no doubt a G-ARBY Special would have been laid on from Exeter to Tipton by now, with tickets on sale in Bristol and Plymouth. This was the TV news story of the week and it had gone nationwide.

The ice cream man rang his bell in Coronation Meadow and children all over the field pestered their parents for twenty pence.

One quick thinking dad said, 'No you can't have one. When they ring the bell it means they are sold out.'

Throughout the Sunday afternoon following the crash there were constantly more than a hundred sightseers in the field.

Sightseers arrive and Annie rakes it in

Anyone with an interest in planes and aviation who lived in the South West was making the journey to Bishop's Court Farm to see the rare sight of a broken Viscount lying in a field. Garby had become a big attraction. By the Tuesday afternoon Annie was able to start selling copies of her own pictures to the visitors. She charged 30p a print and although she had to make regular trips to the chemists in Ottery – the charity collection was coming along nicely!

Garby was lying on level ground at the bottom of the meadow but there is a steep slope of 7.5%, up a twelve metre rise, over the final 160 meters to the gate. The 7.5% slope is a little steeper than 'Cornhill', adjacent to the town church of St Mary's. That is a pretty tough rise if you are towing a Viscount.

Interestingly the Ottery News reported, on the 1st of August, that a 'rail track' had been constructed from near the aircraft, up the slope, to the top gate. I think this is misleading as witness statements and some photographs indicate that the track was constructed of metal planks, linked together, as used by the Royal Engineers to help heavy vehicles move over boggy ground. They were laid at the bottom of the field so that when Garby was raised up sufficiently to enable her own wheels to be lowered to the ground, she could then be towed up to the top of the field where she was to be, in a word used in a popular contemporary film ('Short Circuit'), disassembled. Pictures of the Sparrow's crane, used for the initial and subsequent lifts, show that it is standing on its own large road wheels. That rules out the possibility that the

5.4: Heavy wheels damage Oliver Carter's field.
(Annie Trimmer collection 1980)

track was laid for this crane. The Ottery News also reported that Garby had her 'wings clipped' off on 30th July. This is supported in dated photographs but it is clear from them that only the wing ends were removed, the outer part of the port wing having been almost broken off anyway in the impact with the Lone Oak.

Whilst we are on the subject of boggy ground here perhaps it is as well to record that at least one army truck sank into mud at the bottom of the field and had to be towed out (Pic 5.4). Perhaps there had been some heavy rain in the first two weeks following the landing. This sinking into the mud was understandably annoying to Oliver, John and Sunshine because it caused considerable damage to the soft ground in the area of their carefully constructed drainage system. Oliver was later to successfully claim compensation for this damage.

By the 1ˢᵗ of August, Annie, and her friends had collected more than £400 and had finally decided that all the money would be given to the Stoke Mandeville Hospital, Spinal Injuries Unit. They had heard that Jimmy Savile would soon be in the area and they were hoping to be able to raise at least £800 before the plane was taken away, and present this to Jimmy when he was down their way. People visiting the site had been very generous.

Sightseers continued to arrive from July 19th up until poor Garby was finally taken away in a broken and disassembled state on probably August 11th or 12th (Monday or Tuesday) nearly a month after she had arrived. There is no record of the total number of people who visited Garby in the field but Annie Trimmer estimates the number as probably around 2,000. The farm had become a huge sightseeing attraction and by the first week in August, Kathleen Carter, Pat Cox and Judy Cooper had helped Annie collect £789.

Oliver locks the gate

Two weeks and a few days after the crash, Oliver Carter put up a sign on the gate into the field that attracted a fresh bout of media attention. This he did some time over the first weekend in August, probably when the visitors had gone home on the Sunday evening (3rd August). The reason for its instant newsworthiness was that Oliver was taking on big brother and telling him where to get off. It unambiguously and simply stated: 'STRICTLY NO

ADMISSION'. Why was Oliver upset and was he right to feel that way?

His issue was that, even now, more than two weeks after the crash landing, no one from officialdom, Alidair Scotland, Department of Trade, Air Accident Investigation Branch, Police or any of the other official bodies involved, had asked him this simple question – 'Can we have our plane back please?' Oliver's field was now a well churned-up muddy mess, with army trucks, cranes, tractors and workers crawling all over it every day. No one had even said 'good morning' to him, let alone ask for his permission to start work. He had now had enough of being ignored.

But within an hour of the first official vehicle arriving at the farm on Monday morning (4th August) and failing to access the field, he was rubbing his hands together with some satisfaction. A couple of phone calls to the local press had made sure that this was not going to be a low key lock out. 'They are not coming onto my land,' Oliver told the press.

For good luck, as well as the notice, Oliver made sure that more vehicles could not enter the field by placing a heavy farm tractor, with machinery attached, inside the gate creating a barricade (Pic 5.5). Neither could the vehicles already in the field leave without causing further considerable damage to their own paintwork.

The official reaction was prompt, forthright and predictable. 'He cannot stop us,' The AAIB inspector bristled, 'we have a legal right to go into that field – if he wants to pursue this line it could result in him being prosecuted. We would pass that to the police to deal with.'

As is so often the case in these sorts of situations

EXPRESS & ECHO

Angry Devon farmer barricades Viscount field

NO-GO 'WAR' ON CRASH SITE

5.5: Oliver's barricade.
(Picture; Express and Echo 5/8/80)

officials quickly step in with a heavy hand and a 'don't mess with us' style of response. The truth is probably that Oliver was quite right to be miffed; and let's not forget that he had a hope of achieving compensation for the damage to his livestock and land.

Oliver was his own master on his side of the dispute, but on the other side were several official agencies, not just one. None of these agencies thought sideways for a moment, perhaps understandably, as they had difficult jobs to do as quickly as they could; perhaps they thought that someone else was talking to Oliver. I think most of us would agree that it would have been easy and courteous for one of the AAIB investigators to have called on Oliver sometime on the first day after the crash and opened a dialogue. Everyone needed to co-operate. Politeness costs just a little time but it helps things run along smoothly as every primary school child knows. Anyway eventually Oliver had his dialogue, if not an apology. Having made his point he removed his barricade on Wednesday 6th August. He also later received damage compensation from the Department of Trade and a sizeable payment from Lloyds, the aircraft's insurers.

Oliver had this to say to the press at the time (*re-printed by courtesy of the Express and Echo*).

'Apparently the airline should have written to me and explained all this, but I never received a letter. Even so, I think that the Department of Trade should have consulted me, if only out of courtesy before they went trampling over my land. I did not expect them to call the first night, they were too busy, but I was annoyed when they continued to ignore me. At least barricading the land solved a few points, but I was told if I continued they had the right to confiscate the land.'

5.6: At the top of the field, and awaiting dissection, Garby stands on her own wheels. 4th August, 1980
(*Annie Trimmer, 1980*)

Garby comes apart

The question now exercising the minds of the army engineers who had been tasked with removing Garby from the field was, which bits needed to come off her? This was not a particularly difficult challenge for the Royal Engineers but it did need to be completed tidily and fairly quickly. After all the start of their summer leave was being delayed! All hope of an economic repair had now been abandoned. Garby was to be chopped up and the bits taken to Farnborough to be placed at the disposal of the AAIB.

The first items removed from the plane were the engines, of which number one, the port outer, was already mostly hanging off the wing due to its famous conflict with the staunch, unyielding Lone Oak. Garby was then cradled and lifted by a Sparrows crane; just a few feet off the ground so that her own undercarriage could be lowered. She would be standing on her own wheels – the first time that had happened since her take off from Santander nearly a month ago. It was going to be possible to tow her across the field and up the slope. Not an easy feat but more convenient than chopping her up where she lay.

The army at that time had an impressive, long (39ft) low loader that was quite capable of carrying about half of a Garby – without the wings of course. Two of these were on standby and they were known by the regal and magnificent working title of 'Queen Mary' – presumably named after the large liner of 1936 not the regal consort of King George V who was of slimmer and more ladylike proportions. Anyway, down at the bottom of the meadow all the engineers had to do was to stand Garby up on her own wheels and take the remaining three engines off her.

After the engines were on their way to Farnborough off came most of both wings but the inner sections of the wings were left as they housed the under carriage. Then she was hitched up to a bulldozer and hauled, ignominiously, up the field (Pic. 5.6) – 'and good riddance!' thought the sheep as they stood silently watching. After a few more days of hard work – between the 4th and 9th August – and under the eyes of an undiminishing audience of sightseers, she was in Queen Mary sized pieces and ready for her journey to Farnborough. Her nose and tail were off, as were the stubs of the wings, and her fuselage had been severed at the fifth window (Pic. 5.7). At the top gate, by the lane, she would have the final sections of her wings removed, her fuselage cut in half cross-wise and the sections loaded on to the two Queen Marys (Pic. 5.8).

Annie is on parade

On Saturday 9th of August, Annie was the guest of honour at the Royal Marines Commando Training Centre's Open Day at Lympstone, near Exmouth. Here she met the top brass, watched the Commando displays, listened to the band (Note 5.2) and was applauded by the public for her charitable initiative. Kathleen Carter, Pat Cox and Judy Cooper were with her as invited guests. Annie was thrilled, in front of a large audience, to personally hand to Jimmy Savile her cheque for more than £1,000.

Privately, after the band marched off, Jimmy asked her if he could see the plane for himself on the following day. So on Sunday 10th of August, at the end of the afternoon, he duly arrived at Bishop's Court Farm in his chauffer driven Rolls Royce. After having a look around the plane he signed some autographs and stayed for tea. Everyone was charmed and the collection idea had been a great success.

5.7: Garby severed at the fifth window.
(Annie Trimmer collection)

5.8 and 5.9: Fuselage sections on their 'Queen Marys' and ready for departure. In 5.8 the front fuselage section is on the left.
(Pictures; Annie Trimmer, August 1980)

Garby passes away

On Monday 11th of August the access gate to the lane was being widened to permit the egress of the unusually sized loaded vehicles. The Queen Marys were ready to play their part in the final drama as the severed sections of Garby were loaded. The added width of the gate can still be clearly seen as the hedge is still trimmed to expose its adjusted width. As far as I can see, this, the concentric rings on the Lone Oak, the sliced tree top and possibly the indentation in the field, are the only visible physical reminders of the whole Garby story.

Forlorn, friendless and lonely, her creaking, broken body now torn to bits, she lay on the two Queen Marys. The onlookers, many of whom had watched the surgery of the last few days, were silent and sad to see her go, and who is to say that no tears were shed. The cortege, for that is what it resembled, made its way in a respectfully gentle, dignified and fitting fashion up the lane towards the Salston Manor Hotel and the old town of Ottery St Mary, with its church on the hill, which Garby slowly passed on her way into history.

6

… going, going, gone!

*Inventions here and there / The AAIB Report and the Prunes
/Two Jersey visits / More about Geoffrey Whittaker / Myths /
Some more illuminating, and interesting, bits and pieces /
The Tribute Walk*

Inventions here and there

The previous chapters broadly tell the story of Garby's adventures during the fateful day of the forced landing, 17th July 1980, the build up to that day and what happened to her subsequently. As I explained in the Preface all of the material used has been carefully researched and checked and is, as far as I can tell, true and accurate. However there is some invented material which I class as 'reasonable conjecture'. This material concerns the passengers and conditions in Garby at the time of the incident. My reason for creating and including these ideas was explained in the Preface. I hope they help the reader to feel that he or she is actually on board the plane. If this strategy is successful I will be delighted; it certainly has been fun to write those bits. If it is not successful blame my test readers, who think it works, and I unreservedly apologise!

At the time of writing (July 2018) I still have only been able to communicate with two passengers who were actually on the flight. They are Juan Benjumea and Siobhan Jarrett, the daughter of Mrs Meller. They have given me some useful information, which has largely corroborated my suppositions. Interestingly I am pretty sure that if any more real live passengers or one of the stewardesses do come forward then his or her true story of the day will be much better than my humble conjectures.

Additionally I have invented some dialogue here and there but the invention is always along the lines of 'well she would have said that, or something similar.' Again, that technique I hope brings the situations to life. The invented dialogue certainly does not include the quoted words of Geoff immediately after Garby came to rest and as he was walking through the cabin checking the condition of the passengers.

He was totally convinced that he had not been fuelled properly in Spain. In his own actual, vehemently stated and well witnessed and recorded words immediately after the landing – 'The bastards never filled me up properly!' are exactly what I think he would have said based on all that I have learnt about him. The basic reason for the whole incident is of course centred on the fuel state of Garby as she took off from Santander and that is carefully looked at in the next section of this final chapter.

As I researched and prepared the material, a large number of facts came to light and some of these I find particularly interesting and indeed, curious. There are also several myths to be laid to rest and of course differences of opinion by the witnesses. Add a helping of conjecture and speculation and I expect you will get the general idea behind this final chapter.

There is not room in this necessarily short book for all of those facts and details but I think some of the more interesting ones should be recorded so here they are. We begin with a look at the official verdict on the whole incident – the Board of Trade's Air Accident Investigation Report (9/81). You can easily find the whole thirty-six page document if you go online (Apx 1). I have read the report in full three times during the course of writing this book and have given myself a well-earned chocolate biscuit on each occasion! Do not attempt that at home – the report reading I mean; chocolate biscuits are fine.

The AAIB Report and the Prunes

The Air Accident Investigation Branch (AAIB) report does not give us a clear cut reason for the fuel exhaustion that caused the pilot to make the forced landing. The closest the report comes to giving us an explanation is by stating in its conclusions ((a)(iii)) that 'the port fuel gauge was chronically unserviceable and unacceptable for continued public transport operation: this was a major contributory factor in the accident.' The report also states that the commander should have relied on a dripstick measurement before take off and that only a few litres of fuel were loaded at Santander and also that no reason for this low quantity upload could be established.

Previously the report tells us (para 2.3) that the refuelling vehicle was of a type where it was possible to mishandle the controls in such a way as to produce erroneous indications of fuel delivery. When this was pointed out to senior Spanish officials they expressed surprise and denied that any such mishandling had occurred. There is of course no actual evidence that erroneous indications had been given but equally, no evidence that they had not. What we do know is that not enough fuel was delivered to bring the float valves on Garby into operation as that would have terminated the uplift.

Now I would like you to meet the 'Prunes'; well that's my name for them anyway. They may well be able to help us understand the events of 17th July a little more clearly. They are an online community of expert professional pilots and experienced workers in the air industry. They are actually titled online with the impressive name 'PPRuNe'. They write with clarity and their authority, experience and wide knowledge base is obvious. For example we have the words of the pilot who was flying another Viscount (800 series) on the very same charter on the same day and was actually flying into the landing pattern on the downwind leg at Santander as Garby was taking off on her last flight. He knows the score and that is obvious. You can read his words on the subject easily enough if you go on line to the 'Professional Pilots Rumour Network' (PPRuNe Apx 1) but to save you the trouble I quote his words below.

There are several Prune points that we can look at and I begin with the all-important matter of the fuelling at Santander. The Prunes pick up the point in the AAIB which observes that Garby was filled up before leaving Exeter and if NO FUEL AT ALL had been loaded at Santander then the fuel exhaustion would have occurred just before reaching Exeter on the return trip and within three minutes of the time when it actually did occur. You might like to read that last sentence again as that is probably the reason for the forced landing and indeed also this book. That fact just has to be more than a coincidence.

The next Prune point is that the report also mentions the fact that Garby's recovered Flight Deck Recorder (FDR) showed that as she took off on the fateful last flight she climbed more quickly than she did on the previous flight. This increased rate of climb is consistent with an extrapolated rate if she was lighter by the amount of fuel missing from the uplift. That can be a bit tricky to grasp so in simpler terms try this: she went up faster because she was lighter and that climb rate would have been produced if no fuel had been loaded in Santander. If that was the case she took off with only what was left of the Exeter full uplift minus the fuel used on the outward trip from Exeter, and that was just enough to bring her home, but only as far as East Hill, Ottery St Mary. Oh dear!

After the incident another Prune reports that he demonstrated to his Chief Pilot (not Alidair) that fuel could be pumped around a bowser, clocking up on the meter but not actually loading into the aircraft. The Chief Pilot was amazed and went away to consider how his airline could avoid being a victim of such a malpractice.

For the next point I cannot do better than to give you the exact words of Prune ABUKABOY as written on 14th July 2009 – 'I was right behind him [G-ARBY] on the same set of charter flights, saw him take off as we went downwind at Santander, was the next aircraft to refuel from that very same bowser, but as we were in the Intra 'go-faster' Viscount 815 G-AVJB, we ordered full tanks and didn't stop refuelling until on-board cut-offs worked. Our uplift and OK gauges confirmed our fuel load. Due to a real slick turnaround we caught up with 'BY as we approached Berry Head, and as we took radar vectors for the westerly R/W at Exeter, we suddenly jumped from No 3 to No 2 in sequence on the radio, which seemed a little odd, but we concentrated on the job in hand, broke cloud as we came over the ridge on the ILS in poor light and drizzle, and landed. We taxied in and I was just a little pleased with myself, having just flown my first 'solo' as P1 on the Viscount, and can remember the smile dropping from my face as the handling agent came on the flight deck and broke the news. Exeter was a customs training station and there had been a mega exercise on all day. Guess who were the first to stumble through that field where 'BY' had come to rest? Yup, customs… never mind the state of the passengers, they were there to check the bar-boxes were still sealed! You couldn't make it up!'

Next, an interesting comment on the Prune website from David Eyre who gives us material from his father Peter Eyre, who worked for British Midland and Alidair as Operations Controller and remembers this G-ARBY incident. He writes – 'I was on duty for this crash and remember it very well. People were phoning up asking if I had any lamb chops (as the Viscount had killed some sheep during its belly landing). They had two captains on-board. Conversation after the crash was that as they were overhead Guernsey, they discussed diverting there. The crew thought that if they diverted and if they were wrong about the low fuel state, it would be an acute embarrassment or worse! Many times in both British Midland and Alidair I found a dark cloud over Operations and the crews if they did not attempt to get the aircraft back to its flight-planned destination. It was always a case of commercial pressure versus operational pressure. The other issue is having two captains flying as crew – it could cause some confusion or command challenges during an emergency. Only one captain is P1, but in their minds both are P1. This was the case in another accident at Kirkwall in 1979 with another Viscount (G-BFYZ of Guernsey Airlines), when one captain decided it was okay to land and the other called for an overshoot. Incidentally, this aircraft [refers to G-ARBY] was the oldest flying Viscount in the world at the time. It was the tenth Viscount produced, the second Viscount delivered to Air France, and was twenty-seven years old at the time of the crash. Regards, David Eyre'.

Finally from the Prune website we have an email from Colin Randall published on January 21st, 2009. Colin was a reporter and he had called on Geoff Whittaker in Jersey after the crash but he does not tell us when. He wanted to ask Geoff questions about his dismissal from Alidair. This leads me nicely into the next section and there you can read his piece and also read about my own visit to 'Pont Rose Farm', Jersey (Fix: 6.5), in 2014.

Two Jersey visits

Colin Randall writes; 'Approaching the door of a cottage on Jersey, one of the islands in the English Channel, I was engulfed by ten yelping, leaping Welsh springer spaniels. Anyone who looks after so many of these beautiful creatures is likely to rise in my estimation. But in the eyes of sixty-one other people, their friends and families and the wider public, the man on whom I was calling was already a hero. Twenty-eight years before the "miracle of the Hudson" [US Airways Flight 1549 ditching], Geoffrey Whittaker had averted an air disaster. My thoughts turned to him as I read about the extraordinary events that unfolded in New York after a plane flew into a flock of birds.'

He continues, 'As the pilot of a Bae Vickers Viscount 708, flying fifty-eight passengers plus crew from Santander in northern Spain to the south-western English city of Exeter, Captain Whittaker was confronted by total engine failure eight miles short of his destination. He instantly sent a Mayday distress call, alerted passengers to the emergency and began searching for the least unsuitable place for a crash-landing. It was just after 2050 on July 17 1980. Few on board can have been optimistic of still being alive but Capt. Whittaker brought the plane down with such skill that everyone escaped unhurt. There were two casualties, sheep grazing on the plane's improvised runway, a field that later became a cricket pitch [sic], in the village of Ottery St Mary. Both reportedly found their way into local deep freezers. So why was I, a reporter, visiting the pilot at his island home?… I wished to ask how Capt. Whittaker was getting on in his campaign against dismissal from his job. For the reason the plane had to make a forced landing was that it had run out of fuel. The official accident investigation attributed this to the crew's "erroneous belief that there was on board sufficient fuel to complete the flight". Denied permission to fly, he was concentrating on his dogs, grooming them for competitive shows. What ultimately became of him and his dispute with Alidair, I do not know.' (*Colin Randall's text used with his kind permission.*)

Colin is not completely correct in his observations. There were more than two sheep killed, Coronation Meadow never became a cricket pitch and Ottery St Mary was a town, but these are minor points. I mention the cricket pitch topic in the 'myths' section, and as to what was to become of Geoff's flying career, read on.

I arrived at Pont Rose Farm (Fix: 6.5), which is less than a quarter of a mile south of Jersey's airport, at around 10 a.m. on the 1st of April 2014. Shirley Whittaker greeted me and soon her two black Labradors and four cats were all seeking my attention. Shirley was welcoming and pleased to see me and, after chatting for a couple of hours, we made our way by taxi down to a superb quayside restaurant where we had lunch and continued our conversation. She was very happy to tell me lots about Geoffrey, his career and their life together and I have recorded most of what I learnt in the next section. Shirley, when I visited her, was a fairly sprightly eighty-seven-year-old and we both enjoyed our time together talking about her fondly remembered husband who had sadly passed away in August 2009. She told me a little about herself and I discovered that she came from Penarth, near Cardiff and was born there in 1927. After World War II she served in the Princess Mary's RAF nursing service in Aden and it was there that she met Geoff in 1955.

After lunch we returned to Pont Rose Farm where I was able to present her with a commemorative gift from the Ottery St Mary Heritage Society and take some photographs of some of Geoffrey's keepsakes, including sections of his log books (Pic: 6.1).

More about Geoffrey Whittaker

We are now going to look a little more closely at the hero of our story, and I am quite happy to call him a hero because although the whole sorry business would have been avoided if he had physically checked the fuel levels before take off, he did a magnificent piece of flying as he adeptly executed the forced landing. No pilot could have done more. He was undoubtedly a hero in the minds of all of the passengers and he was fêted and praised by the press and media in the days after the incident. But what sort of a man was he? I introduced him in chapter 2 and we learnt a little of his 'flying start' and war time work but now, with the main story told, we can take a closer look.

June	25	724	RC	Jazi	P₁.	16+
	28	724	RC	..	..	105
	29	724	RC	..	..	073
July	2	724	RC	..	..	114
	16	708	BY	..	..	093
	17	708	BY	..	..	1400
1981.						
Dec.	4	BN4A	WR	LAF	MORRIS	04
Dec	30	BN III	YO	..	P₁.	082
DEC	30	BN III	YO	..	..	194
Dec	31	BN III	YO	..	..	1215
Dec.						

6.1: Captain Whittaker's log book, showing July 80 and 1981 dates.
(Shirley Whittaker collection).

6.2 (below): In the log book shown above, Geoffrey has written on the July 17 line, after the 1400 on the right 'Force Land!!' but could it be read as 'Free Lamb'?
(Shirley Whittaker collection).

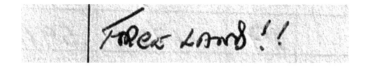

It is not easy to imagine just how it must have felt to have been the pilot of an aircraft flying a Transport Command mission in World War II. A lot of the flying was predominantly long, boring hours of keeping on course and looking forward to a hot meal of some sort when they arrived at their distant destination. The repatriation flights he flew for prisoners of war from Japan must have been particularly arduous. Through the active years of the war up until 1945 there was always the threat of enemy attack and many RAF transport aircraft were shot down. In an attack suddenly guns would be blazing, the plane twisting, turning, sometimes tumbling and taking violent, evasive action. Geoffrey would always have been half expecting such an attack. At night dazzling lights would disorientate and confuse even the most experienced flyer. He experienced situations in which, in the previous week, friends were lost – more will go down next week, shot to bits – but tonight, I'm lucky – I'm always lucky. This is the war Geoffrey had survived. It was no wonder that there was a 'devil may care' facet to his personality.

6.3: Below: Geoffrey Whittaker in his MGTC. Aden, c. 1955
(Shirley Whittaker Collection)

6.4: TheWhittakers and some of their dogs. circa 1978
(Shirley Whittaker collection)

He felt, without actually ever saying the words, 'Well I came through that lot – everything else is a walk beside the river.' He started off each flying day with an optimistic view of 'It'll all be fine. That's the way it always is for yours truly! So why bother to check the dripstick? After all it's not in the company regulations. Of course she has all the fuel she needs to get us home. We'll be fine.'

His attitude towards the necessary administrative work of a pilot was perhaps not always quite up to the mark. Colleagues who knew him well described him as being an excellent pilot but not such a good captain. At Exeter, where he was well known, he once trained some new pilots on a 'Britten-Norman BN2 Islander aircraft' and the forthcoming

144

endorsements in the pilots' licences were invalid because Geoffrey's TRI (Type Rating Instructor) qualification had expired.

For much of his career as a commercial pilot he was often away from home, but for some of that time he was based in Jersey. At home his main interests away from flying were dog breeding, boating and golf, and he enjoyed cooking meals at home for himself and Shirley. He was also a prominent member of the Masonic Lodge in Jersey and that enabled him to do a considerable amount of useful charitable work. He was a sociable man and had lots of friends in Jersey and in the international aviation community. He took great pride in his labradors and spaniels, and these were exhibited and won prizes at many dog shows (Pic 6.4). Perhaps they were taking the place of children because sadly the couple were unable to have children due to one of the several cancers that Geoffrey had during his life. How they would have loved to have had a family there on Jersey.

Geoff and Shirley had fallen for each other when they were both working in the RAF in Aden in 1955. Shirley likes to tell the story of an event that took place one sunny afternoon on the shores of the Arabian Sea. Geoffrey owned an impressive little MG sports car (Pic 6.3) and he had taken Shirley on a spin down to the beach. On the way back to base she recalls that they were travelling at speed on a quiet road with bends when the steering linkage broke. Geoff called out, 'I have no steering – hold on!' They crashed into the entrance gate of the French Embassy, which caused a bit of a stir and altered the appearance of the front of the MG a little! They were married early in 1956 at the imposing church which Shirley knows as 'top church', in her home town of Penarth, South Wales.

As he was approaching the time when he was about to be discharged from the RAF, Geoffrey had the unusual appointment of Liaison Officer for the Empire Games, which were held in Cardiff at the end of July 1985. The RAF obviously thought very highly of our Geoffrey.

When I asked Shirley what she remembers about the forced landing at Ottery St Mary she said that she had been badly shaken by the event.

'It was so unusual for Geoff to have anything go wrong whilst flying… ' she told me. 'On the night of the event I was desperate to talk to him and have him tell me what had happened but every time the phone rang it was another pushy reporter. They were heartless really. My husband might have been dead. All I knew was that there had been a crash.

'Eventually, after hours,' Shirley continued, 'he told me everything was alright… it wasn't of course, but at least he was alive. He told me that he was demanding a bowser dip at Santander, but I didn't really understand what he meant. I do now. He told me that the plane was always in and out of the hangar with the faulty fuel gauge but they could never fix it.'

Geoff came home at the weekend and in the following week lots of letters arrived congratulating him on his flying. He was cross about the whole situation and knew that he was going to lose his job. Not to have been able to fly again would have destroyed him as it was the most important thing in his life.

I was interested to learn what happened after Geoffrey had stopped flying for Alidair. Was that the end of his flying career? Shirley said, 'You can look at his last log book and see for yourself.'

So there I sat at her kitchen table surrounded by cats, dogs and mementos looking at the captain's log books. What a thrill it was for me, after reading so many press cuttings and tramping around the muddy meadow back in Ottery, to sit there with Shirley with the 'July 17th' entry open in front of me, and I have my photograph of the page open in front of me as I write. It simply says across the columns; 'July 17 708 BY 1400 XTR-SDR-XTR 4.20 FORCE LAND!!' (Pic 6.2). It's easy enough to work out what all that means and it might well have also meant that Geoffrey Whittaker would never fly again, but that was not to be the case. The following year, after spending some time working as a radio operator on 'Ship to Shore' communications at Corbiere (SW Jersey), Geoffrey was back in the air as a commercial pilot. His log book shows that on 4th December 1981 he was flying on a 'Middle East Route' around the Gulf (Pic 6.1). He was on a two week on/off cycle and on one of these duties he was scheduled by his airline to fly King Hussein of Jordan around the Middle East States. The king obviously took a shine to Geoffrey, or at least thought that his soul was in mortal danger, because in thanks for his good work the king gave Geoffrey a large Bible bound in Mother of Pearl and a big picture of himself also bound in Mother of Pearl – the picture that was, not the king! Shirley gave these precious items to the Masonic Lodge in Jersey but she thinks they have been lost.

6.5: Geoffrey and his sister at Pont Rose Farm, Jersey. c.2004
(Shirley Whittaker collection)

Myths

The plane landed on the cricket pitch

The myth concerning the cricket field (Fix 6.4) is very simple and very full of nonsense. This was the first myth I encountered when I became interested in the Garby story. In fact it was that simple statement that aroused my interest.

I am a great fan of the website Google Earth and if you have not discovered it and you have internet access you really should have a close look at its wonders (Apx 1). The whole planet has been photographed digitally from space and with a bit of practise you can be zooming in to see your back garden in no time. What a wonderful thing it is – not your garden, Google Earth. Pictures can be taken and placed by the users and I have placed several at the locations relevant to the Garby events. In my initial investigation I looked at the Ottery St Mary cricket field from above and saw clearly that there is barely enough room to land a helicopter and certainly not a charging airliner. The closest Garby probably came to the field was overhead at the south-east corner, around one hundred feet above the ground.

GW never flew again after the forced landing.

Well he certainly did, as his log books show. (See the last paragraph of the previous section above.)

GW knew where to land the plane

'He did not,' says Shirley, his wife, and 'It is likely that he didn't,' say my pilot experts. The idea that he had previously 'spied out the land just in case' is nonsense according to the pilots. The pilots I talked to as I prepared the earlier chapters said that big airliners do not land in fields, they can only land on runways of at least firm, level grass and generally land on a tarmac surface. It is such a remote chance that a pilot could land on rough, uneven ground that they do not even train to do so. However it certainly is the case that Geoffrey knew the topography to the south of Ottery St Mary. He could see where his best 'forced landing' options lay and he could also see that he was not going to get over West Hill. It is true that GW knew the approach to Exeter Runway 27 very well for he had landed there hundreds of times.

Wheels up is standard practise in a forced landing.

No. The pilot will make his own best decision. Wheels down would have the slight advantage of absorbing some of the impact energy before the wheels are smashed off by the rough ground. If the wheels had been down whilst Garby was in the air more drag would have been created and Geoffrey would not have wanted that. He made a quick and sound decision to go in 'wheels up'.

He picked the only place to land.

Ouch! No, no, no! With no power, he was not doing much picking at all. There was only a little choice but it does look as though he could have continued straight along parallel with the western edge of the Alder Grove rather than making the dog leg, left then right, turn. He would then have had a straight run between the trees and missed the Lone Oak. You can see this possibility in Google Earth. Though if his progress on the ground had not been adjusted for him by the Lone Oak he might have careered over the ground so fast that he would have piled into the railway embankment and big trees near the far corner of the field.

It wasn't a 'crash' at all.

This is a bit of a semantic, nit picking myth. People have generally jumped down my throat when I have casually asked something like, 'Do you know about the 1980 air crash?' The AAIB refers to events as a 'forced landing', so do all the pilots who have assisted me and consequently I have generally done the same, but in my book, if a bit of a plane smacks into an oak tree at nearly a hundred miles an hour that qualifies as a good, old fashioned 'crash' as well!

At the very end the pilot turned the aircraft left to stop it hitting the railway embankment.

No. The impact with the Lone Oak turned the plane to the left. From the moments immediately before ground impact Geoffrey had no control of the aircraft.

The Viscount 708 flew on four propeller engines.

Well it certainly looked like that most of the time but in fact the engines were turbo prop, that's a jet engine also turning a propeller. That is a very clever idea and it first appears in the Viscount (Type 630, 16th July, 1948). Amazingly it only needed one of those engines to be producing power to keep it in the air – and of course some fuel!

The OSM fire brigade was soon on the scene

Sorry, not so. In fire brigade terms, twenty minutes – being generous – is hardly 'soon'. This was looked at in detail in Chapter 4 but the myth exists because the press stated '… they were at the plane… within three minutes of touchdown'. I say they were not and so do all the witnesses.

There wasn't enough fuel

There was, but it puts us firmly into the 'what-ifs'. If GW had declared an emergency at his east of Berry Head position – which we have to estimate (Fix 6.1) – because he became convinced that he was nearly out of fuel, he could have told Exeter control that he was taking a west to east approach on runway 09. The wind was light, we know that because a light drizzle was falling. The time saving would have been around nine minutes and the fuel saving 276 litres; easily enough fuel to land in the other direction, and then even a short taxi.

However on the negative side, and against a west to east landing, is the Exeter heavily built up area in the last few miles of the approach, high ground to the west and the fact that the approach aids for 09 were not as good as those for 27. On balance of course Geoffrey was absolutely right to attempt to land from the east, but there was enough fuel to reach safety although he did not know that.

Some more illuminating and interesting bits and pieces

The Salston Hotel

As the Salston Hotel plays such an important part in the Garby story it is worth mentioning a little of the relevant history. When Garby arrived on 17th July 1980 the hotel was owned by Neils and Elizabeth Svendsen, and they had owned it for about ten years but they sold it, probably in 1981, to the Best Western Group. The manager was Martin Dowse and he bought the place from the previous owners probably in 1991 and he maintained the business until the end of 2007. At the time of writing (July 2018) the hotel is derelict but a two-year re-development has commenced. Sadly Elizabeth Svendsen died in 2012; a kind and generous lady who played a major part in the events in her hotel on the night of the landing.

Donkeys were kept in a paddock beside the lane. Before the present 'new' entrance and drive were built the access drive ran down the slope and along the front of the hotel to the main entrance. The interest of the Svendsen family in donkey rescue led eventually to the creation of the nearby Donkey Sanctuary (Fix 6.2).

Alan Nicholl, our witness in Chapters 3 and 4, tells us that he remembers seeing one of Garby's prop blades prominently on display and highly polished, in a glass case in the hotel's foyer and that this was often the subject of enquiries from arriving guests.

Peter Harris has a call

I want to mention Peter Harris again here mainly because of an interesting event that happened to him, we think in 2010. One day he had a telephone call from a man in the Oman who said that he was on board a plane that crash landed in a field near Ottery St Mary. He had seen a press article that had mentioned Peter and he had been able to track him down. The man said his father was with him on the plane

6.6: Peter Harris holds one of Garby's bent propeller blades.
(Picture; Jim Rider, 2014)

and that he had taken a movie film from the cockpit. He then went on to say that he would soon be in England and that he would like to meet up with Peter so that Peter could tell him some more facts about the incident.

Peter said, 'I would be delighted to meet you. Just ring me when you are here and in the area.' Peter never heard any more from the man and as he had no contact details from him, contact was lost. Let's hope the caller makes contact again. I would also be pleased to meet him. Incidentally Peter also has a Garby prop blade in his garage, which serves him mainly as a 'history room' (Pic 6.6). It was good to be able to hold the prop, heavy though it was, when I visited him. Peter witnessed Garby passing overhead and that is reported in Chapter 3.

ITN footage

There is footage held by ITN and it is quite probable that this includes the 8mm footage mentioned by the caller in the Peter Harris section above. The website charges a fee if visitors want to see or use the footage.

Other clips show the plane on the ground at around ten o'clock on the evening of the crash – the Alidair Scotland signage is clearly visible – and another clip is an interview with Geoff Whittaker as he walks down beside the Alder Grove pointing out the crash site and saying that he hopes to be able to fly commercially again in the future. This was taken months after the crash, possibly when he attended Pixie Day with Shirley the following year (1981).

Alidair – some more information

According to the Aviation Safety Network (Apx 1), the Alidair airline was established in 1972 and ended operations in 1982. During the latter years of its operations the company owned thirteen aircraft but of course that total did not include G-ARBY. The company was owned by Roger Dadd and we think that in March 2015 he was still alive. The Brittany Ferries charter during which the fateful flight for Garby occurred was typical of the wide ranging work that the company undertook. No doubt the loss of Garby – and Viscount G-BFYZ (see next paragraph) – had a fairly major impact on the company finances.

The Aviation Safety Network also lists another Alidair aircraft, Vickers 735 Viscount G-BFYZ, as being involved in an incident that resulted in a total write off. This crash occurred at Kirkwall Airport in Orkney on 25th October 1979 and the crew of four and forty-seven passengers were lucky to escape with their lives when in rough weather with gusting cross winds number 4 propeller (outer starboard) struck the runway. The cause for the crash was given in the official report as an 'unstable approach' and an unreliable windscreen wiper. As the AAIB reports do not name the pilot we do not know who the Alidair pilot was. When I asked Shirley Whittaker if it might have been Geoff she said, 'I don't know about that crash but I don't think it was Geoff. He would have told me.'

A press article concerning the final Garby flight, which I am unable to identify, published shortly after the forced landing reports that Captain Treford Jones, Vice Chairman and joint MD of Alidair said, 'The aircraft [took off] with more than the minimum fuel requirement under British Civil Aviation Authority rules. We are at a loss to understand why the fuel warning lights came on and why the engines cut. Each engine has its own fuel supply.' Well it is obvious now that the take off fuel state was way below the minimum requirement and the warning lights came on because the fuel gauge system was well known to be faulty and was listed as such in the technical log. Well obviously a Vice Chairman doesn't have to concern himself with minor details!

The Stephen Morrin Book

On the 10th May 2002 the Sidmouth Herald reported that a Mr Stephen Morrin had visited the Salston Manor Hotel and met several of the witnesses already mentioned in this book. Mr Morrin's aim was to gather information for a book – possibly to be titled 'Plane Truth' – describing twelve post war air accidents and that it was to be published in 2003. Stephen's most popular published work is 'The Munich Air Disaster' and his website (Apx 1) mentions, somewhat inaccurately, some of the details of the Garby incident and also shows him holding a Garby propblade, well… resting it on the ground; at least I managed to pick it up! We have been unable to trace a published book by him on the G-ARBY story but it might well be out there somewhere and worth reading.

Pulmans' News Cutting

An undated cutting from a Pulmans News published a few days after the landing reported Geoff Whittaker as saying '… the landing did not feel too bad and I was very sorry that four sheep were killed…' He also paid tribute to the passengers and crew saying 'they were magnificent.'

He also praised the rescue services that arrived within minutes. Then he told the reporter about the aircraft itself '… the Viscount, which was Britain's bestselling airliner ever, was a pioneer among turbo prop aircraft and had an excellent safety record. The first flew thirty-two years ago and 440 of the machines were sold all over the world. It was the best plane I have ever flown. Its handling made the job of the forced landing that much less difficult.'

Pulmans also reported in the same edition that many of Oliver Carter's valuable racehorses were kept at Bishops' Court Farm, including his 1976 Gold Cup winner 'Ottery News'. Men quickly rounded up the terrified horses after the crash.

Move the flight path

In the week following the landing the Ottery News of 25th July dutifully reported the rather excitable exchanges that had taken place at the local council meetings. 'FLIGHT PATH MUST BE MOVED', thundered the headline and continued thus… 'the crash landing of a Viscount has led to angry demands that the flight path into Exeter Airport be changed. The plane skimmed low over Ottery St Mary before landing in a field. The vicar of Ottery St Mary, the Rev Peter McGee, said, "the plane came so close to hitting Ottery St Mary but didn't. It was a miracle!" The call for the flight path to be moved has been backed by Mr Niels Svendsen, proprietor of the Salston Manor Hotel.'

Later Councillor Tom Fraser of OSM told a meeting of the East Devon District Council '... a disaster was averted by the sheer skill of the pilot. The plane passed over the rooftops of many houses, clearing them only by a matter of feet. One does not begin to think what would have happened if the plane had landed on the town.'

He also said that the flight path should be moved either north or south, so that planes did not fly over populated areas. He also asked if more fool-proof checks could be carried out to ensure that aircraft had enough fuel aboard to reach their destinations.

The chairman said the question would be discussed at the next meeting of his committee. He said the subject of more vigorous fuel checks was not in the council's jurisdiction. On Sunday in churches throughout the area, prayers of thanks were said for the escape of the passengers, crew and residents.

Well there is quite a lot to think about there; I am particularly amused by the 'miracle' concept! The point about the flight path however is worth a serious comment and it is this; flight paths into airports lead straight to the end of runways – bends are definitely not required – the general idea being to safely line up the plane onto its touch down point in the same direction as the runway. The main runway itself has to be built into the direction of the prevailing wind. There aren't any real alternatives to that except 'no runway means no airport.' Some would perhaps like that, but airport locations are a matter of national policy and the argument in favour of the South West having reasonable access to national and international flights will win the day, any day.

As the flight path over Ottery is actually only directly overhead just eight houses – in the Meadow Close and Butts Road area (Fix 6.3) – it is a bit extreme to suggest that the entire population of Ottery is at risk of annihilation. I agree that Garby flew over quite a few houses but, after all, if the worst came to the worst, Geoffrey would have been quite able to push her down into one of the many surrounding fields and probably kill only those on board. Certainly the Salston Manor Hotel, and its occupants, were lucky to have survived the incident. The flight path today is as it was in 1980, with the slight adjustment that Runway 27 is now 26 (and in the other direction of course, 09 is now 08), but that has absolutely nothing to do with Ottery St Mary being where it is and everything to do with the prevailing wind and the location of Exeter.

Where is that baby now?

What a pity it is that so far we have only been able to make contact with two of the passengers on the flight. Peter Harris came close to success when he did actually speak to another passenger – if only we knew which one and where he is now.

Wouldn't it be wonderful if I could tell you what happened to Mrs Muriel Quartermain of Oxford's baby, the one that was to be called Geoffrey. Bad luck if 'he' turned out to be a 'she' though. And where are those two magnificently cool stewardesses, Sandra and Sue? They made such a positive contribution to the incident and the passengers, and those of us interested in the story, would like to know something of what happened to them subsequently.

... and finally... The Tribute Walk

As the idea for the book took shape and I found myself thinking of Garby as a person rather than as a collection of manufactured parts and mechanical bits and pieces, I felt that she was leading me on to tell her story as fully as I could. I think of her now as perhaps an engine driver might think of his steam engine; she was a living, breathing person with a beating heart, much the same as you and me. So I was not surprised when the idea came along that I might make my own personal tribute to her on the anniversary of her last flight. I thought also that I might actually write the last sentences of this tale right there, where she came to rest, exactly to the minute, thirty-eight years previously. That is what I did and those final words are below as the last paragraph of this chapter.

So there I was, on my own, at 2053 on the 17th July 2014, standing on the old railway embankment as close as I could be to where Garby finished her long slide across

Coronation Meadow. The reasons for my tribute were simple: firstly – Garby had hung together when she needed to do so and as a result no one was badly hurt – surely a tribute to British engineers who built the best aircraft in the world in the 1950s. Secondly – Geoffrey flew magnificently, as he had done in World War II. Thirdly – on the ground at and near the landing site lots of people demonstrated kindness and decency when their help was needed. The Viscount, and the landing, were things to celebrate and events might well have taken a different course.

It was a dry evening so far but heavy, threatening rain clouds were moving slowly in from the west as I parked my car soon after 2010 at St Saviours' Bridge and walked down beside and along the old railway embankment. Occasionally I looked up, half expecting Garby to come whistling along, and eventually, down at the crash site, I stood for a minute, silent and still and imagined her sliding quickly towards me over the rough ground sideways, scattering sheep.

Along came one man and his dog, out for their evening walk. I thought that a picture would be a good idea so that I could remember the scene and asked him if he would take it for me. He kindly did and here it is for you to see (Pic 6.7). I gave him a very brief account of the reason that brought me there to the embankment and I told him a little of the remarkable Garby story. He told me that he was a teacher at a local primary school and this was quite a coincidence because one of the reasons for writing the book was to keep the story alive and make it available to young people. I thanked him for his help and with his dog running ahead, along beside the river, off they went.

None of us would ever want to be in a 'Garby-like' situation that's for sure, but if by some mischance we were, it might be a good idea to do what is always a good idea during life's rough times and that is to keep cool, hang on and trust that you will be as good at flying in the face of danger as was Geoff Whittaker. 'You can do it,' Bill had told him.

On the way back up to the bridge and the safety of my car, the most almighty thunderstorm erupted above me and shook all the trees in the Alder Grove and rattled the windows in the deserted and decaying Salston Manor Hotel. Sheep gathered under the trees, lightning flashed all across the sky and I was soaked through as I ran, slipping and sliding over the last few hundred yards to my car. Garby had provided me with a final spectacle, nature in the raw and a never to be forgotten experience.

If you are ever down there beside the River Otter and on the old railway embankment, passing Coronation Meadow at 2053 on the 17th July any year, you might just spare a thought for Garby, Geoff, Bill, Annie, Sandra and the others, and you might even meet another 'Garbyist', for that is what you now are as you have read this little book, and for doing so, I thank you.

6.7: Jim Rider beside Coronation Meadow.
The Lone Oak is clearly visible.

Notes and References

Notes on the text

Chapter 1 Going South

As a general note – if the reader is able to access Google Earth I suggest that it is a good idea to visit it frequently as you read through the book. See the 'Links to websites' in Appendix 1 for the web address.

1.1 In this book G-ARBY, the official registration, is usually called 'Garby' for the reasons given in the Preface.

1.2 The runway is now (2018) identified as '26'.

Chapter 2 Going North

2.1 The AAIB report 9/81 is discussed in Chapter 6.

Chapter 3 Going down

3.1 AAIB Report 9/81: The height of the ground above mean sea level (ASL) at the Bradshaw-Smith bungalow is 56m and Charles was looking up at Garby, about 90 feet above him. Height (ASL) for other locations in the area are; East Hill (on Garby's probable path) 251m: Lone Oak 35m: nose final position 34m.

3.2 A 'Giving Set' is a medical apparatus used for fluid administration in an emergency.

3.3 The Nightingale Nurses are named after Florence Nightingale. They were trained at St Thomas' Hospital, London, or one of its successor hospital training schools. They provided nursing care at many hospitals in the UK, particularly in the London area.

3.4 G-ARBY did not stall. Without going into too much technical detail, an aircraft (fixed wing) is said to be 'in a stall' when it is going too slowly to fly. To generate enough 'lift' to keep the plane up, the pressure on the lower surface of the wing must be greater than that on the upper surface. This is achieved because the lower surface is flat and the upper surface curved. Pilots are trained to avoid stalls and in the unlikely event of one occurring the pilot knows how to recover the aircraft to normal flight. G-ARBY was always above the stall speed as she glided into impact.

3.5 There are concentric rings, as if they had been drilled, at about the impact height of the No. 1 engine. I asked Edwin Locke if he had noticed this when we stood together, looking at the tree. 'No I haven't,' he said. 'Well I certainly didn't drill it,' he added. See the picture on page 72.

3.6 A sagittal section divides the body on a vertical plane into right and left halves. The sheep was cut straight through from its nose to tail.

Chapter 4 Going nowhere

4.1 Lilly Lock is Edwin 'Sunshine' Locke's mother. The difference in spelling was caused at Edwin's registration (for a reason unknown).

4.2 Oliver Carter did not live here.

Chapter 5 Going away

5.1 Readers can contact the Ottery St Mary Heritage Society for updated information about the G-ARBY incident. To contact them see (Appendices; Links page 174). If you were on-board G-ARBY and involved in the incident, or have knowledge of someone who was, they would be delighted to hear from you.

5.2 The author was the Director of Music of the Band of HM Royal Marines Commandos from 1987 until 1990.

List of Locational Fixes (Grid references)

Fix Name (Co-ordinates) and notes

1.1 Wisley Airfield (51°18.397N 0°27.486W)

1.2 Garby's final position (50°43.998'N 3° 17.344'W) on 074 Degrees.

1.3 Runway 27 at Exeter Airport (50° 44.179'N 3° 24.047'W)

3.0 Slade Close (50° 45.081'N 3° 16.010'W) Nicholl family lived here in 1980.

3.1 Grandisson Drive (50° 45.024'N 3° 16.175'W) Peter Harris lived here in 1980.

3.2 Playing Field (50° 44.892'N 3° 16.902'W)

3.3 Salston Manor Hotel (50° 44.512'N 3° 17.453'W)

3.4 Bradshaw-Smith family home (50° 44.478'N 3° 17.512'W) Bradshaw-Smith family lived here in 1980.

3.5 Alder Grove (50° 44.318'N 3° 17.420'W)

3.6 Access gate (50° 44.174'N 3° 17.654'W) into Coronation Meadow from lane to/from Tipton St John.

3.7 Tree top sliced off (50° 44.250'N 3° 17.334'W) also see pic.

3.8 Garby hits the Lone Oak (50° 44.109'N 3° 17.384'W)

3.9 Number 1 engine impacts the ground half a second before Garby's belly impacted the ground at (50° 44.154'N 3° 17.381'W)

3.10 Garby final position of nose (50° 43.998'N 3° 17.344'W)

4.1 Top Field gate (50° 44.364'N 3° 17.514'W)

4.2 Fire Station 1980 (50° 45.107'N 3° 16.673'W)

4.3 Bishop's Court Farm (50° 44.034'N 3° 17.750'W)

4.4 White Cross view point (50° 42.951 N 3° 15.586'W)

6.1 Off Berry Head (50°22.333'N 3°18.544'W). Turn right for shortcut to Beer Head and then to Runway 27 or left for an approach to Runway 09.

6.2 Donkey Sanctuary (50°41.817'N 3°11.427'W). Donkeys were originally at Salston Manor.

6.3 Meadow Close and Butts Road (50°45.380'N 3°16.453'W) Flight Path to EXD 27/26 is overhead.

6.4 OSM Cricket field (50° 44.804'N 3° 17.250'W)

6.5 Pont Rose Farm, Jersey. (49° 12.043'N 2° 11.500'W)

Appendices

Appendix 1

Sources and links to websites

Classic Civil Aircraft: 4 VICKERS VISCOUNT by Alan J Wright. Published by Ian Allan Publishing ISBN 0-7110-2070-1

Handbook of the VICKERS VISCOUNT by P St. John Turner ISBN 7110-0052 2

Links to websites (correct in 2015)

Airliners.net Link;
http://www.airliners.net/aircraft-data/stats.main?id=380

Pictures of VISCOUNTS
www.vickersviscount.net/Pages_Photos/Photos_
    CNGallery.aspx
Vickers Viscount specifications, pictures, and data. Find
    photos, information and specs for the Vickers Viscount,
    www.airliners.net/aircraft-data/stats.main?id=380

Pictures of VISCOUNTS and other planes
www.airplane-pictures.net/type.php?p=180

Air Accident Investigation Report No. 9/81
www.aaib.gov.uk/cms_resources.cfm?file=/9-1981%20
    G-ARBY.pdf

'Ottery St Mary Heritage Society'
www.otteryheritage.org.uk/

The Professional Pilots RumoUr NEtwork
www.pprune.org
PPRuNe (Good discussion on G-ARBY) (often referred to
in the text as 'the Prunes')
www.pprune.org/archive/index.php/t-379916.html

Google Earth
www.google.com/earth/download/ge/agree.html

Aviation Safety Network (ASN)
http://aviation-safety.net/database/record.php?id=1979102
    5-0

S Morrin book on G-ARBY (unpublished?)
www.aidan.co.uk/photo7726.htm

Appendix 2

The Viscounts – more information

In 1943, in the dark days of World War II, the British Government had set up the 'Brabazon Committee' to make recommendations about the future of the British aircraft industry and how it could avoid being dependant on American aircraft companies after the war which, by the way, it assumed Britain would win. Amongst other recommendations the committee identified a need for a medium range turbo-prop airliner and gave specifications. The Viscount was created by Vickers in response to those recommendations.

The magnificent, newly developed Rolls Royce turbo-prop engines, of which there were four, were able to deliver an unprecedented amount of thrust for an engine of its weight and size. Simply explained, a 'turbo-prop' has a jet power unit driving a turbine shaft with a propeller in front. On this first 'test build' aircraft the engines were early 'Darts' but later, on the main production 700 series models, the 'DART Rda 3' was fitted.

With the experience gained at Weybridge from the trial and development of the 600 series, and careful market research, Vickers knew that the world's airlines with medium length routes, of around 250 to 600 miles, needed an aircraft with more passenger capacity. Designers set about developing the 700 series, which was ultimately to have up to seventy-one seats. With the increase in capacity came an inevitable increase in everything else. The aircraft's dimensions increased, now to a span of 28.56 metres and a length of 24.77 metres, and larger engines were developed by Rolls Royce who continued to be steadfastly loyal to the Viscount project. A completely new fuel system was developed as was the vitally important de-icing system for those chilly altitudes, particularly over Canada. In order to help keep their integrity under pressurization, cabin windows were elliptical with three or four on each side doubling as emergency exits.

The first occasion on which one of the new 700 series Viscounts flew as part of a fully scheduled service occurred on Saturday 29th July, 1950. Taking off from Northolt Airfield, London, the flight landed at Paris', Le Bourget. During the 1950s the 700s became increasingly popular with airlines operating UK domestic and European routes. Development and improvement continued at the Vickers' works at Weybridge and BEA successfully opened Viscount services to many European destinations including Rome, Athens and Cyprus.

In all a total of around 440 Viscounts were built between 1948 and 1964. These were constructed initially at the Vickers' establishment at Weybridge and then, with large orders continually rolling in from many operators around the world, a new construction centre was added at Hurn

Airport near Bournemouth. At the peak of production in the latter 1950s, ten aircraft were being built each month. Revenue for Vickers exceeded £177,000,000, a spectacular income for any British company at this time.

By the end of 1951 Viscounts were flying from hundreds of airports, including most European countries and Rhodesia, Argentina, Paraguay and India. With this wide diversity of ownership, Vickers continued to make parts available and was always happy to help with technical and service enquiries from operators. However, maintenance and management by foreign airlines was not always as it would have been in Britain and Europe, and a relatively high number of incidents are recorded in the 1950s and early 60s. One source quotes a total of 145 crashes, many involving fatalities.

Despite serious competition from Boeing, and a natural tendency in the USA to promote their own companies, many operators there saw the advantages of economy offered by the British turbo-prop Viscounts. In 1952 Air France ordered twelve Viscount 708s and one of these was later to become G-ARBY. She was built by Vickers as Constructor's number 10 and delivered to Air France as F-BGNL on the 25th of August, 1953. By the end of 1952 the 700s, and later the larger 800 series, Viscounts were in the skies over most of the USA and Canada. Trans Canada Airlines carried more than 470,000 passengers in Viscounts in the first year of use alone and considerably increased their profits as a result.

The USA airlines caused a few headaches at Vickers' HQ when a total of 250 modifications to the British version were demanded. These included air conditioning, as flights often included southern routes to 'hot' states. ALL NIPPON AIRWAYS, the Japanese airline, introduced the flying public to in-flight TV viewing when the first television sets were first mounted on seat backs in the 1960s. At the time of writing there is a preserved Viscount V701 (G-ALWF in BEA colours) on display at the Imperial War Museum (Aircraft), Duxford, Cambridgeshire (CB22 4QR).

The larger 800 series of Viscounts first took to the skies in July, 1956 and production of the 700s was phased out. Production of the Viscount ceased in 1964. Vickers saw the lifespan of a Viscount as around thirty years and the key factors governing 'end of life' as the total number of landings and the durability and integrity of the pressurization system. The stress caused to the airframe by continual pressurization and landings eventually weakens the structure to an unsafe level. When the aircraft were withdrawn from main route operations they were often bought or leased by charter companies for lower altitude freight or special passenger work. G-ARBY was one of many aircraft which flew in the colours of several operators. It was eventually bought by Alidair, a charter company based at the East Midlands Airport, Castle Donnington, Derbyshire, in 1975.

Appendix 3

G-ARBY PEOPLE (54)

BAKER, George	Ambulance Service	Devon
BEAN, Michael	Passenger	G-ARBY
BEAN, Mrs	Passenger	G-ARBY
BEAN, Mrs (senior)	Passenger	G-ARBY
BEAN, child	Passenger	G-ARBY
BEAN, child	Passenger	G-ARBY
BENJUMEA, Juan	Passenger	G-ARBY
BENJUMEA, Pilar	Passenger	G-ARBY
BENJUMEA, Juan (child age 13)	Passenger	G-ARBY
BOYES, John	Eye-witness	Fluxton
BRADSHAW-SMITH, Jeremy	Doctor	Salston Manor
BURNS, Paul	Managing Director	Brittany Ferries
CARTER, Oliver	Farm manager	Fluxton field
CARTER, Katherine	Fundraiser	Fluxton
COOPER, Judy	Fundraiser	Fluxton
COX, Patricia	Fundraiser	Fluxton
DADD, Roger	Chairman	Alidair

EVANS, Colin	Chief Supt.	Exeter
FEATHER, Peter	Hotel Manager	Salston Manor Hotel
FISHER, Anthony	Ambulance crew	Honiton
FRASER, Tom	Town Councillor	Ottery St Mary
HARRISON, Russ	Eye-witness	Metcombe
HAWKINS, Edgar	Station Fire Chief	Ottery St Mary
HAYES-FITTON, Christianne	Passenger	G-ARBY
HILL, Nicola	Manageress	Salston Manor Hotel
HICKOCK, A. J. ('Wild Bill')	Co-Pilot	G-ARBY
HUDSON, Sue	Stewardess	G-ARBY
IKIN, Peter	Vet	Ottery St Mary
JONES, Trefor	Joint MD & Captain	Alidair
KILLORAN, John	Chief Fire Officer	Devon
LOCK, Lilly	Eye-witness	Fluxton
LOCKE, Edwin ('Sunshine')	Eye-witness	Fluxton
MATTHEWS, Harold	Passenger	G-ARBY
MATTHEWS, child	Passenger	G-ARBY
MATTHEWS, child	Passenger	G-ARBY
McCULLOCH, Stuart	Guest	Salston Manor Hotel
MARALES, Wanda	Passenger	G-ARBY
McNEIL, Sandra	Stewardess	G-ARBY
MELLER, Patricia	Passenger	G-ARBY
MELLER, Siobhan	Passenger	G-ARBY

MELLER (?), Partner of Patricia	Passenger	G-ARBY
MORGAN, Brian	Asst. Chief Constable	Exeter
OSMAN, Jill	Passenger	G-ARBY
QUARTERMAIN, Muriel	Passenger	G-ARBY
QUINDIMIL, Maria Pilar	Passenger	G-ARBY
ROBERTS, Andrew	Chef	Salston Manor Hotel
ROWLAND, Jeff	Eye-witness	Salston Barton
SELLICK, Robin	Passenger	G-ARBY
SVENDSEN, Niels	Owner	Salston Manor Hotel
SVENDSEN, Elizabeth (Betty)	Owner	Salston Manor Hotel
TRIMMER, Annie	Eye-witness	Fluxton
VASQUEZ, Maria	Waitress	Salston Manor Hotel
WHITTAKER, Geoffrey	Captain	G-ARBY
YOULDEN, David	Farm worker	Ottery St Mary

Total passenger breakdown
20 Passenger names are known.
Passengers were:
19 adult male,
24 adult female,
13 children,
2 infants. Total: 58

1.2: Viscount V701 cabin c.1980. G-ALWF, photographed at Duxford.
(Picture; Jim Rider 2014)

Appendix 4

Passenger Seating (known and unknown people)

Some known, some best probability.

1A	1B	1C	Aisle	1E	1F
2A		Marales, Wanda	Aisle	USA man	USA woman
3A Bean child	Mr Michael Bean	Mrs Bean	Aisle	Mrs Bean senior	Bean child
4A Van boy	Van dad		Aisle	Van mum	Van girl
5A Mrs P Meller	Meller (husband)	Meller, Siobhan	Aisle		Sellick Robin
6A (wing)	Osman, Jill	Hayes-Fitton, Christianne	Aisle		6F(wing)
7A (wing)	Matthews, child	Matthews, Harold	Aisle	Matthews, child	7F (wing)
8A (wing) Benjumea, Juan (13) son	Benjumea, Juan	Benjumea, Pilar	Aisle		8F (wing)
9A			Aisle	Canadian man	

183

10A Elderly Lady 1	Elderly Lady 2	Quartermain, Muriel	Aisle		Quindimil, Maria
11A Office girl	Boy friend		Aisle		
12A DOOR	NO SEAT	NO SEAT	Aisle		
13A Sue Stewardess	Sandra Stewardess		Aisle	NO SEAT	NO SEAT

Appendix 5

History of Viscount 708 G-ARBY
Provided by Chris Saunders

1953 Built by Vickers as Constructor's Number 10 and delivered to Air France as F-BGNL on 25/08/53. Operated on Air France European routes.

1960 Sold to Maitland Drewery on 07/06/60 and re-registered as G-ARBY.

1961 Leased to Danish Air Charter.

1961 Leased to Silver City Airways.

1962 Operated by British United Airways, after taking over Silver City Airways.

1966 Sold to Air Inter and re-registered F-BOEC. Used on French internal routes.

1975 Sold to Alidair on 07/08/75 and reverted to G-ARBY.

1975 Leased to Dan Air until 1977, and sub-leased to Cyprus Airways during 1975.

1977 Reverted to Alidair colours, and used on charter flights.

1980 Written off at Ottery St Mary, Devon on 17/07/80.

Appendix 6

Armorique and G-ARBY timeline
15/7/80 – 18/7/80 all times in BST

Day/Time	Armorique	GARBY	Comments/events
Tues. July 15th			
0700	Depart; Plymouth	–	
1100	Engine fails	–	Discussions begin
1500	Arrive; Roscoff	–	Santander; Brittany Ferries office is busy. Charter aircraft (3) booked. Disembark all passengers at Roscoff. Repairs start.
Wed. July 16th			
1700	Repairs in Roscoff going well.	–	Brittany Ferries advised
2300	Depart; Roscoff	–	In service
Thurs July 17th			
1630	–	Arrive; Santander	Crew only. 2nd flight of the day
1500	Arrive; Santander		Embark some passengers
1800	Depart; Santander		With some passengers and vehicles
1833	–	Depart; Santander	To OSM only
2053	–	Forced landing	
Fri. July 18th			
1400	Arrive; Plymouth		With some passengers and vehicles

Appendix 7

Timeline of key events on 17th July 1980
By Jim Rider; Feb 2015

Time	Key Event	Note
1833	G-ARBY takes off at Santander	Flight QA 7815
2028	G-ARBY turns right at Berry Head	Heading for Beer Head
2050	All Engines stop due to fuel starvation	Mayday sent
2051	Jan and Alan Nicholl and Peter Harris see G-ARBY glide past	
2052	Bradshaw-Smith family see G-ARBY glide past	Charles BS sprints after G-ARBY
2052	Les Carter sees the 'plane low, passing left to right.	Then he drives after it, south along Strawberry Lane, passing Salston Hotel.
2053	G-ARBY completes a forced landing	Coronation Meadow, Bishop's Court Farm
2055	Emma BS phones Emergency services, then runs to gate into field arriving by 2107	She is unable to give the emergency services an exact location now of the aircraft.
2056	Charles BS arrives at G-ARBY	
2056	News of crashing airliner spreads in OSM	
2056	Les Carter arrives in top field.	Watches events at the 'plane for about (estimate) twenty minutes, then departs back up his route down the lane. Does not see a fire engine.
2057(est.)	Edwin Locke arrives at G-ARBY	
2058 (est.)	Frank Bastin leaves his house for the Fire Station by motorbike.	Arrives soon after 2103(est.)
2058 (est.)	Jeff Rowland arrives at G-ARBY	
2103 (est.)	Nicholl family to 'White Cross' Where they see flashing blue lights coming from 'all directions'.	Arrive 2108 (est.)
2107 (est.)	Annie Trimmer rounds up the horses	With Anna. Sees an ambulance arrive but does not recall a fire engine.
2108 (est.)	An ambulance arrives at the field gate.	Probably from Sidmouth
2110 (est.)	Fire Brigade departs Ottery SM G-ARBY	
2112 (est.)	Dr. Jeremy BS arrives at G-ARBY	Having collected his medical equipment. Does not see a fire engine.
2115 (est.)	Fire Brigade arrives at G-ARBY	

Appendix 8

More about IFR (Instrument Flight Rules) relating to the flight of G-ARBY (17/7/80). Basic information.

Generally speaking, all commercial flights, regardless of the aircraft size or speed, operate under IFR – 'Instrument Flight Rules'. Under these rules the No.1 altimeter in aircraft when at or above something called a Transition Altitude (TA), which varies from area to area but is generally between 3000' and 6000' must be set to an international standard figure of 1013 millibars /29.92 ins and aircraft must fly at Flight Levels (FLs). This ensures that altimeters are being read off the same correct base setting and this is also the altimeter setting in meteorology which is compliant with the 'International Standard Atmosphere' – the ISA.

In order to fly IFR the aircraft has to carry a certain minimum level of equipment and the commander has to have a Current Instrument Rating (CIR), which is type specific for the Viscount in this case, and issued by the Civil Aviation Authority (CAA) of whichever country issued his Pilot's Licence (PL).

The airspace is divided into various FIRs (Flight Information Region) controlling well defined airspace and the flight is usually passed from FIR to FIR as it travels its route. All of the FIRs on Garby's flight plan would have received the 'Flight Plan' details and would know what to expect. Today, inside controlled airspace, airways and 'Flight Information Regions' – with the help of modern technology – the aircraft is usually monitored on radar but that was not widely available in 1980.

Now flights are often re-assigned 'Flight Levels' by controllers and sometimes radar headings are given en-route too, usually to shorten the route by cutting a corner. This is now possible because the passage of aircraft is monitored much more effectively with modern radar. Radar identification is made by the 'Transponder' in the aircraft which gives out a numbered 'squawk'. This appears on the radar screen so that the controller can see exactly which aircraft it is and where it is, how high it is and whether or not it is deviating from an assigned course or 'Flight Level'. Outside controlled airspace there are rules concerning altitudes to be flown and, as previously explained, there is the regulation called the 'Quadrantal Rule' which lays down various height bands for various directions of travel. The modern TCAS (Traffic Collision Avoidance System) works on transponder transmissions, predicts possible conflict and gives the pilot avoidance instructions but again this was not in use in 1980.

Near miss

There are all too frequently incidents of 'near misses' recorded in UK and adjacent air space. The Civil Aviation

Authority reports that in 2011 there were twenty-two incidents involving commercial aircraft in near misses. Alarming? Yes it certainly is. Big planes, known as 'heavies' have very tight laws, rules and procedures which should keep them in the right place and away from other aircraft. To be precise these aircraft should never be within 1,000 feet of vertical separation from another aircraft and within five miles of horizontal separation. Unless they are landing or taking off, big heavy aircraft will be above 9,000 feet and smaller, piston engine 'air taxi' class will usually operate at between 5,000 and 9,000 feet. Little planes by the way, and broadly speaking, have to keep 500 feet away from anything else, be it on the ground or in the air, and must conform to 'procedures' and generally stay below 10,000 feet. But a little plane in the wrong place can be a big problem for a big plane in the right place. Every pilot has to stick to the same rules. The horizontal and time separation between big and small becomes really important on final approach when the wake turbulence from a 'heavy' can completely spoil the light aircraft's day!

Appendix 9

More about Flight Planning

When making flights such as Garby's, aircraft follow 'highways in the sky' known as 'Airways'. Most of this route, from Cognac VOR to Berry Head, is along 'airway A25'. The pilot flies towards beacons that send out a radio signal on a fixed frequency. The 'not-flying pilot' tunes the navigation radios to these as the flight progresses. Other aircraft will also be using the same airway so when there are lots of flights things will be busy. A bit like the M25 but in three dimensions, with aircraft above and below each other but a separation system of 1,000 feet keeps them safely apart. As well as that if you are in an airway tracking between 000 degrees and 179 degrees you have to be on an 'odd' number altitude – like 17,000 feet – and if you are going the other way you will be on an even number – 18,000 feet. It is obviously important that each aeroplane keeps at their correct altitude (Flight Level) and keeps within the bounds of the airway, which is ten miles wide. Airways start at a particular 'Flight Level' and extend upwards, usually to as high as any aircraft would fly. As an example, the A25 Airway starts at Flight Level 65 and is tagged on the chart as

'FL 65' – 6,500 feet on the International Standard Altimeter setting of 1013 millibars. A pilot certainly needs a head for figures as well as a head for heights.

The Use of the Teleprinter in 1980

Most young pilots flying commercial aircraft around the world now will never have heard of a 'Teleprinter' and will trust now in much more sophisticated forms of online communication. The Teleprinter dates from the second half of the 19th Century and after a hundred years of development was, by 1980, quite up to the job but it was soon to be on the electronic scrap heap.

Appendix 10

More about Fuel Management

In order to calculate how much fuel an aircraft needs for a flight the pilot takes into account lots of factors. Just for fun and to help you get the idea of how this bit works, here is a light-hearted look at what a car driver would have to do if he was using the same system as used by a pilot.

Imagine our motorist is planning to drive from Exeter to London. Before leaving he wants to take on board the minimum fuel he requires because he does not want to waste his money carrying more weight around the place than he needs. Also he might well be a bit short of ready cash. The ground rules for this game are that he must keep driving until he reaches his destination or a diverted destination; he is not allowed to stop and he cannot take on any more fuel. Then he must assume that roads are closed and he must divert and stop a fair way off his route, like the Isle of Wight or Birmingham, or go back to his start point. He next assumes that when he is nearly at London he has to drive around roads for an hour just to use up some time. He has to take more spare fuel for another hour's driving and then, just for luck, he adds up all that so far and then adds another 5%.

He can, of course, deduct any fuel he already has in the tank but to check how much he has he must use the fuel gauge which, unless he is very unlucky, will be working nicely, unlike Garby's. On the plus side for the motorist compared to the aviator, all the fuel units will now be measured in litres, not gallons on the forecourt and litres in the tank, and not weighed out in pounds (as in 'lbs').

Most people could work that out in about ten minutes over a cup of coffee but, of course, no one ever does. Pilots do the equivalent all the time or they have their computers do it for them.

Appendix 11

List of photographs, diagrams and illustrations

Diagrams

Photographs

Acknowledgements and Credits

When I started researching material for this book it soon became obvious that I needed some help. Fortunately I have a long suffering wife, Linda, who is well used to my new projects, foibles and grumpiness if things don't go my way! It was to her I initially turned for assistance with 'just a little research'. Four years later she is still at it!

Chris Saunders, from the Ottery St Mary Heritage Society, was a stalwart and unfailing helpmate with his meticulous cataloguing and industrious ferreting in the archives. Off he went to Plymouth Museum, Duxford War Museum, the Internet and anywhere else he thought would be productive. He had many contacts in the Ottery St Mary area and these proved invaluable and a font of information.

John Allison, whom I regard as my Chief Pilot advisor, with his comprehensive knowledge of all things 'airliner' has been remarkable. Nothing has been too much trouble for him; a quick question or a detailed account of how flight planning worked in 1980; he has given me just the right amount of information just when I needed it.

It was a great pleasure to meet Shirley Whittaker at the home she had shared with Geoff at 'Pont Rose Farm' in Jersey. Shirley was charming, helpful and she willingly shared a lot of her memories with me. She also allowed me to photograph some of her treasured possessions and mementoes of her husband. I am most grateful to her for her help and co-operation in the preparation of this book.

I have discovered that a book like this cannot be written without the help of lots of people and I am deeply indebted to all my helpers. I hope that the list below names them all because I do want them to know how very much I have appreciated their work, unfailing support, encouragement and friendship. It has been an immense pleasure to work with them all and I hope that they enjoy seeing the fruits of their labours in print.

Jim Rider
Honiton,
July 2018.

My experts, family, friends and helpers. Thank you.

Allison, John. Aircraft information. Air Law and systems, ground staff expert, bowser systems.

Bastin, Frank. Witness – Fire Service – site information.

Beeston, Mike. Aircraft information. Air Law and systems, Commercial Pilot.

Benjumea, Juan. Passenger. Information.

Boyce, John. Witness – site. Information.

Bradshaw-Smith, Ann. Witness – site. Reader.

Bradshaw-Smith, Charles. Witness – site and flight. Reader.

Bradshaw-Smith, Dr Jeremy. Witness – site. Reader, advice, pictures and cuttings.

Brady, Catherine. Honiton. Information.

Brady, John. Honiton. Idea for book. Research. Reader.

Brittany Ferries (Christopher Jones). Plymouth. Information.

Chapman, Clare. Gittisham. Research. Reader.

Clark-Lewis, Peter. Aircraft information. Air Law and systems. Commercial Pilot.

Corry, Jane. Sidmouth. Contact information. Advice.

Devon & Somerset Flight Training Dunkeswell. Advice, guidance, contact information.

Express and Echo Exeter. Permissions. Pictures.

Forth, Ann. Fluxton. Information.

Gibbons, Paul. Information.

Giles, Chris. Duxford. Imperial War Museum. Viscount guided tour. Information.

Google Earth. Website Images.

Hands, David. Duxford. Imperial War Museum. Viscount guided tour. Information.

Harris, Peter. Witness – flight. Pictures and press cuttings.

Hawkins, Edgar. Witness – site. Fire Service information.

Jarrett (Meller), Siobhan. Passenger. Information.

Jones, Christopher. Brittany Ferries Information.

Lea, Adrian. Curious Otter Bookshop Ottery St Mary. Information and guidance.

Lock, Lilly. Witness – site. Reported in press.

Locke, Edwin. Witness – landing. Information.

Locke, Pam. Witness – site. Reported in press.

Mowll, Andrew. Exeter. Contact information. Advice.

Neal, Robert. Ottery St Mary Heritage Society. Advice and guidance. Information.

Nicholl, Alan and Jan. Witnesses – flight. Contact information.

Ottery News. Information. Pictures.

Plymouth Library. Research, advice, guidance. Information.

PPRuNe (members) website Information.

Pulmans Weekly. Permissions. Pictures.

Rider, Anthony. Research sources. Information. Air Law.

Rider, Linda. Research. Information. Reader. Advice. Proofing.

Rider, Martin. Research. Information.

Saunders, Chris. Ottery St Mary Heritage Society. Research, advice and guidance. Information. Reader.

Smith, Roger. Pictures.

Trimmer, Annie. Witness – site. Information. Reader.

Wakefield, Chris. Ottery St Mary Heritage Society. Advice and guidance, book design and publishing.

Ware, Mike. Pictures.

Watts, Dr James. Studio pictures.

Watts, Thomas and Matthew. Ideas. Information.

Whittaker, Shirley. Information. Pictures.

About the author

Jim Rider has lived in east Devon since 1987 and retired as a Director of Music in the Royal Marines in 1994. He served as Her Majesty The Queen's Director of Music in *HM Royal Yacht Britannia*. On his retirement from the Royal Marines he set up and managed his own very successful music education service in more than sixty West Country schools.